STEALING INNOCENCE

Youth, Corporate Power, and the Politics of Culture

Henry A. Giroux

palgrave

STEALING INNOCENCE
Copyright © Henry A. Giroux, 2000. All rights reserved. No part
of this book may be used or reproduced in any manner whatsoever
without written permission except in the case of brief quotations
embodied in critical articles or reviews.

First published 2000 by
PALGRAVE™
175 Fifth Avenue, New York, N.Y. 10010 and
Houndsmills, Basingstoke, Hampshire RG21 6XS.
Companies and representatives throughout the world.

PALGRAVE is the new global publishing imprint of St. Martin's
Press LLC Scholarly and Reference Division and Palgrave Publishers Ltd (formerly Macmillan Press Ltd).

ISBN 0-312-22440-0 hardback
ISBN 0-312-23932-7 paperback

Library of Congress Cataloging-in-Publication Data

Giroux, Henry A.
    Stealing innocence : youth, corporate power, and the politics of
culture / by Henry A. Giroux.
        p. cm.
    Includes bibliographical references and index.
    ISBN 0-312-22440-0 (hardback) 0-312-23932-7 (paperback)
1. Culture—Political aspects. 2. Politics and culture. 3. Children
and adults. 4. Education—Aims and objectives. 5. Free enterprise.
6. Industries—Social aspects. 7. Civil society. I. Title.

HM621.g57 2000
00-042075
306 21—dc21
CIP

A catalogue record for this book is available
from the British Library.

Design by Acme Art, Inc.

First paperback edition: May 2001
10 9 8 7 6 5 4 3 2 1

Printed in the United States of America.

STEALING INNOCENCE

ALSO BY HENRY A. GIROUX

Ideology, Culture and the Process of Schooling (1981)

Curriculum and Instruction: Alternatives in Education, edited with Anthony Penna and William Pinar (1981)

Theory and Resistance in Education (1983)

The Hidden Curriculum and Moral Education, edited with David Purpel (1983)

Education Under Siege: The Conservative, Liberal, and Radical Debate Over Schooling, co-authored with Stanley Aronowitz (1985)

Schooling and the Struggle for Public Life (1988)

Teachers as Intellectuals: Toward a Critical Pedagogy of Learning (1988)

Critical Pedagogy, the State, and the Struggle for Culture, edited with Peter McLaren (1989)

Popular Culture, Schooling & Everyday Life, edited with Roger Simon (1989)

Postmodern Education: Politics, Culture, and Social Criticism, co authored with Stanley Aronowitz (1991)

Postmodernism, Feminism and Cultural Politics: Rethinking Educational Boundaries, edited by Henry Giroux (1991)

Igualdad Educativa y Diferencia Cultural, co-authored with Ramón Flecha (Barcelona, Spain: 1992)

Border Crossings: Cultural Workers and the Politics of Education (1992)

Living Dangerously: Multiculturalism and the Politics of Culture (1993)

Education Still Under Siege, second edition; co-authored with Stanley Aronowitz (1994)

Between Borders: Pedagogy and Politics in Cultural Studies, edited with Peter McLaren (1994)

Disturbing Pleasures: Learning Popular Culture (1994)

Fugitive Cultures: Race, Violence, and Youth (1996)

Cultural Studies and Education: Towards a Performative Practice, edited with Patrick Shannon (1997)

Counternarratives, co-authored with Peter McLaren, Colin Lankshear, and Mike Cole (1996)

Pedagogy and the Politics of Hope: Theory, Culture, and Schooling (1997)

Channel Surfing: Racism, the Media, and the Destruction of Today's Youth (1998)

Critical Education in the New Information Age, co-authored with Manuel Castells, Ramón Flecha, Paulo Freire, Donaldo Macedo, and Paul Willis (1999)

The Mouse That Roared: Disney and the End of Innocence (1999)

Juventud, Cultura y Educación, co-authored with Peter McLaren (Madrid, Spain, 1999)

Impure Acts: The Practical Politics of Cultural Studies (2000)

To Susan, my dearest love and companion.

To Jack, Chris, and Brett who are always in my heart.

To John DiBiase, my fallen comrade.

*To Linda Barbery, a sister that Gramsci
would have loved.*

*To Stanley Aronowitz, Donaldo Macedo, Roger Simon, and
Bill Reynolds—national treasures
and brothers to the end.*

*To working class kids everywhere—learn,
dance, and organize!*

CONTENTS

ACKNOWLEDGMENTS

All writing is a collaborative project, and I am particularly grateful to friends such as Larry Grossberg, Carol Becker, Randy Martin, Micaela Amato, Don Schule, Stanley Aronowitz, Donaldo Macedo, Roger Simon, Paul Youngquist, David Theo Goldberg, Jeff Nealon, Cheryl Glenn, Heidi Hendershott, Lynn Worsham, Ralph Rodriguez, Eric Weiner, Susan Searls, Lee Quinby, and others for their support and critical feedback on this project. Susan Searls and Eric Weiner were particularly helpful in reading and editing the manuscript. I also want to thank Sue Stewart, my administrative assistant, for all of her excellent support. My editor, Michael Flamini, graciously supported this project from the beginning. Alan Bradshaw is an outstanding production manager and his input has made a qualitative difference in the manuscript. I would particularly like to thank Meg Weaver for her incredible copyediting of the manuscript. She really made a qualitative difference in shaping the work. I also want to thank my students for all of their feedback, help, and critical advice.

The essays which appear in this book have been extensively revised and in large part bear little resemblance to the originals. They have been previously published in: "Nymphet Fantasies: Child Beauty Pageants and the Politics of Innocence," *Social Text* 16:4 (1998), pp. 31-53; "Heroin Chic, Trendy Aesthetics, and the Politics of Pathology," *New Art Examiner* (November 1997), pp. 20-27; "Rethinking Cultural Politics and Radical Pedagogy in the Work of Antonio Gramsci," *Educational Theory* 49:1 (Winter 1999), pp. 1-19; "Radical Pedagogy and Prophetic Thought: Remembering Paulo Freire," *Rethinking Marxism* 9:4 (1996/97), pp. 76-87.

Childhood Innocence and the Politics of Corporate Culture

> Children are the future of any society. If you want to
> know the future of a society look at the eyes of the
> children. If you want to maim the future of any society,
> you simply maim the children. The struggle for the
> survival of our children is the struggle for the survival
> of our future. The quantity and quality of that survival
> is the measurement of the development of our society.
> —Ngugi Wa Thiong'O, *Moving the Centre: The Struggle for*
> *Cultural Freedoms*

INTRODUCTION

This book explores the seemingly separate but interrelated nature
of three myths, all of which function to limit substantive democracy, the welfare of children, and socially engaged scholarship. The
first myth, "the end of history," assumes that liberal democracy has
achieved its ultimate victory and that the twin ideologies of the
market and representative democracy now constitute, with few
exceptions, the universal values of the new global village.[1] Within
this myth, liberal culture becomes synonymous with market cul-

ture, and the celebrated freedoms of the consumer are bought at the expense of the freedoms of citizens. Little public recognition is given to either the limits that democracies must place on market power or how corporate culture and its narrow definition of freedom as a private good actually may threaten the well-being of children and of democracy itself. In short, the conflation of democracy with the market cancels the tension between market moralities and those values of civil society that cannot be measured in strictly commercial terms but that are critical to democratic public life. I am referring specifically to values such as justice, respect for children, and the rights of citizens.

The second myth, "childhood innocence," is constructed around the notion that both childhood and innocence reflect aspects of a natural state, one that is beyond the dictates of history, society, and politics. In this commonsense conception, children are understood, as cultural theorist Marina Warner suggests, as "innocent because they're outside of society, pre-historical, pre-social, instinctual, creatures of unreason, primitive, kin to unspoiled nature."[2] Marked as innately pure and passive, children are ascribed the right of protection but are, at the same time, denied a sense of agency and autonomy. Unable to understand childhood as a historical, social, and political construction enmeshed in relations of power, many adults shroud children in an aura of innocence and protectedness that erases any viable notion of adult responsibility even as it evokes it.[3] In fact, the ascription of innocence largely permits adults to not assume responsibility for their role in setting children up for failure, for abandoning them to the dictates of marketplace mentalities that remove the supportive and nurturing networks that provide young people with adequate healthcare, food, housing, and educational opportunities.

The third myth, "disinterested scholarship," embodies the legacy of an ever-expanding commercial culture that harnesses the capacity for public dialogue and dissent to market values. This pervasive commercial culture is also seen in the modern obsession with careerism and specialization and in the isolation of educators from politics and the pressing demands of civic life. This third myth suggests that teaching and learning are no longer linked to improving the world; the imperatives of social justice are surrendered to a fatalism that renounces practical politics in order to accommodate the academic culture of professionalism and the ideology of disinterested scientific investigation. Postcolonial theorist Edward Said insightfully comments on the twin dynamics of accommodation and privatization. Each dynamic informs disinterested scholarship and the culture of professionalism at all levels of education:

> By professionalism I mean thinking of your work as an intellectual as something you do for a living, between the hours of nine and five with one eye on the clock, and another cocked at what is considered to be proper, professional behavior—not rocking the boat, not straying outside the accepted paradigms or limits, making yourself marketable and above all presentable, hence uncontroversial and unpolitical and "objective."[4]

The increasing isolation of academics and intellectuals from the world around them reflects corporate culture's power to define teaching as a technical and instrumental practice rather than as a moral and political act. Removed from the world of practical politics and everyday life, many educators are all too willing to renounce culture as a distant terrain of politics and struggle. Buttressed by the pressures of disinterested scholarship and its attendant calls for neutrality, objectivity, and rationality, this approach offers little room to consider how ideologies, values, and power shape all aspects of the educational process. As British cultural theorist Richard Johnson points out:

> Teaching and learning are profoundly political practices. They are political at every moment of the circuit: in the conditions of production (who produces knowledge? for whom?), in the

knowledges and knowledge forms themselves (knowledge according to what agenda? useful for what?), their publication, circulation, and accessibility, their professional and popular uses, and their impacts on daily life.[5]

But mainstream discussion of education not only ignores the ideological nature of teaching and learning, it also excludes culture from the political realm by enshrining it either as a purely aesthetic discourse or as a quasi-religious call to celebrate the "great books" and "great traditions" of what is termed Western Civilization.[6] In both cases, any attempt to transform the nation's classrooms into places where future citizens learn to critically engage politics and received knowledge both inside and outside the classroom are dismissed as either irrelevant or unprofessional.

I argue throughout this book that the politics of culture provide the conceptual space in which childhood is constructed, experienced, and struggled over. Culture is the primary terrain in which adults exercise power over children both ideologically and institutionally. Only by questioning the specific cultural formations and contexts in which childhood is organized, learned, and lived can educators understand and challenge the ways in which cultural practices establish specific power relations that shape children's experiences. While popular sentiment holds that culture, especially popular culture, either does not matter politically or educationally or that it does not represent a dire threat to children, I provide in the second section of the book a number of theoretical approaches based on the work of political theorist Antonio Gramsci, educational theorist Paulo Freire, and cultural theorist Stuart Hall. These approaches view culture as crucial to any serious forms of politics and pedagogy that seek to engage the current assault on youth. I discuss some of these issues at the end of this introduction.

At first glance, these three powerful mythologies appear to have little in common; yet I attempt to demonstrate throughout this book that it is impossible to invoke one in any meaningful way without invoking the others. What links these three seemingly disparate mythologies? Quite a lot, I believe: In their deployment they (1) excuse the adult world from any responsibility toward youth by appealing to a thriving economy and the natural order and by denying the political and cultural roles that educators and education play in children's lives; (2) reproduce race, class, and cultural hierarchies; and (3) limit citizenship to a narrowly privatized undertaking. What all three myths ignore is the increasingly impoverished conditions that future generations of youth will have to negotiate. Childhood is not a natural state of innocence; it is a historical construction. It is also a cultural and political category that has very practical consequences for how adults "think about children"; and it has consequences for how children view themselves.[7]

THE POLITICS OF INNOCENCE

In our culture, the most persistent image of the innocent
child is that of a white, blond-haired, blue-eyed boy . . .
and the markers of middleclassness, whiteness, and
masculinity are read as standing for all children.
—Henry Jenkins, "Introduction: Childhood Innocence and
Other Myths," in the *Children's Culture Reader*

On one hand, by claiming childhood innocence to be a natural as opposed to a "constructed" state, adults can safely ignore the power imbalance between themselves and children; after all, if children exist beyond the pale of adult influence, then they have neither agency nor rights, except to be constrained or protected from aberrant outside forces.[8] On the other hand, the myth of childhood innocence is a way of denying the effects of real social problems on children and also a way for adults to shift attention away from the pressing problems of racism, sexism, family abuse, poverty, jobless-ness, industrial downsizing, and other social factors that make the end of the twentieth century such a dreadful time for many adults and especially for children, who are often powerless in the face of such forces.[9]

When adults cling to the idea that a thriving free market economy, with its insidious consumer-based appropriation of freedom and choice, provides the greatest good for the greatest number, they diminish "the role of politics in public life in favor of an exclusive focus on individual experience—on a politics of personal responsibilities and self-interest rather than one of the collective good."[10] This view makes it easier for adults to claim that social problems are individual problems. This claim, in turn, allows them to downsize the public sphere, eliminate government-funded safety nets for children, and substitute punitive policies for socially invested legislation. In this approach, the logic of the marketplace blames kids—especially those who are poor, Latino, or black—for an alleged lack of character while it dismantles social services that help to meet their most basic needs. Without understanding the experiences of actual children, contemporary society confronts the sometimes perilous, although hardly rampant, consequences of drug use and violent behavior by stiffening jail sentences for teens, trying them as adults, and increasingly building new prisons to incarcerate them in record numbers.[11]

What complicates the intersection of these myths—the end of history, childhood innocence, and disinterested scholarship—is the way in which they erase the exploitative relations of class, race, and gender differences even as they reproduce them. For example, the appeal to innocence by conservatives and liberals alike offers protection and security to children who are white and middle class while defining the condition of their innocence within the racial-, class-, and gender-coded "traditional notions of home, family and community."[12]

Public reactions to the 1999 killings at Columbine High School suggest how innocence is expressed along racial and class lines. The comments of the residents of Littleton, Colorado were widely reported in the press. The residents laid claim to the racially coded legacy of innocence by proclaiming that "It couldn't happen here" or "This is not the inner city."[13] *The Nation* columnist Patricia Williams argues that such comments reflect "innocence profiling," a practice often associated with privileged white kids who, in spite of their behavior, are presumed to be too innocent for their criminal behavior to be treated seriously. According to Williams, the two teenage killers, Dylan Klebold and Eric Harris,

> seem to have been so shrouded in presumptions of innocence— after professing their love for Hitler, declaring their hatred for blacks, Asians and Latinos on a public Web site no less, down- loading instructions for making bombs, accumulating the ingre- dients, assembling them under the protectively indifferent gaze (or perhaps with the assistance) of parents and neighbors, stockpiling guns and ammunition, procuring hand grenades and flak jackets, threatening the lives of classmates, killing thirteen and themselves, wounding numerous others and destroying their school building—still the community can't seem to believe it really happened "here." Still their teachers and classmates con- tinue to protest that they were good kids, good students, solid citizens.[14]

Williams's claim that the myth of innocence protects privileged white kids seems legitimate: the national press was dumbfounded that the two teenage gunmen, given their affluent backgrounds, could have murdered twelve fellow students and a teacher before taking their own lives. One TV reporter in Columbine referred to one of the killers as "a gentleman who drove a BMW."[15] Other media accounts emphasized how much promise these boys had, attributing their criminal behavior largely to temporary psycholog- ical conditions. They were described as alienated, pressured, and stressed out—terms seldom used to describe the criminal behavior of nonwhites.

Unlike crimes committed by youth in urban areas, the Columbine massacre prompted a nation-wide soul searching over the loss of childhood innocence and the threats faced by white children in affluent areas. Senate Majority Leader Trent Lott (R-Miss.) called for a national conversation on youth and culture. Sociologist Orlando Patterson challenged the dominant media response to Littleton and the racially coded notion of innocence that informed it. He asked in an op-ed column in *The New York Times* what the public response would have been if "these two killers had not been privileged whites but poor African-Americans or Latinos." He responded that "Almost certainly the pundits would have felt it necessary to call attention to their ethnicity and class."[16] Actually, Orlando's comments are understated. If these kids had been black or brown, they would have been denounced not as psychologically troubled but as bearers of a social pathology. Moreover, if brown or black kids had exhibited Eric Harris and Dylan Klebold's previous history of delinquent behavior, including breaking into a van and sending death threats to fellow students over the Internet, they would not have merely been given short-term counseling. On the contrary, they would have been roundly condemned and quickly sent to prison. But since white middle-class communities cannot face the consequences of their declining economic and social commitment to youth, they generally give their children the benefit of the doubt, even when their troubling behavior veers to the extreme. White middle-class children often are protected by the myth of innocence and are considered incapable of exhibiting at-risk behavior. And if they do exhibit deviant behavior, it is often blamed on the "alien" influence of popular culture (now often synonymous with hip-hop) or other "outside" forces—well removed from the spaces of "whiteness" and affluence.

Innocence, in this exclusionary rhetoric, is highly discriminatory and generally does not extend its privileges to all children. In an age extending from Ronald Reagan to George W. Bush, the notion of innocence does not apply to certain children and is being renegotiated for others.[17] Historically poor kids and children of color have been considered to be beyond the boundaries of both childhood and innocence; they have been associated with the cultures of crime, rampant sexuality, and drug use. In fact, they are quite often perceived as a threat to the innocence of white middle-class kids who inhabit increasingly fortress-like suburbs, shielded from the immorality, violence, and other "dangers" lurking within ever-expanding multiethnic cities.[18] When dealing with kids whose lives do not fit the Ozzie and Harriet family profile, middle-class adults invoke the antithesis of innocence. In short, the rhetoric of innocence and its guarantee of support and protection typically have not applied to kids who are poor, black, and brown. There is evidence that this idea changed in the 1990s; while minority youth are seen as utterly disposable, now white suburban kids increasingly face the wrath of adult authorities, the media, and the state.[19] As anthropology theorist Sharon Stephens cogently argues:

> There is a growing consciousness of children *at risk*. But the point I want to make here is that there is also a growing sense of children themselves as *the risk*—and thus of some children as people out of place and excess populations to be eliminated, while others must be controlled, reshaped, and harnessed to changing social ends. Hence, the centrality of children, both as symbolic figures and as objects of contested forms of socialization, in the contemporary politics of culture.[20]

Although some children are seen as "at risk," more and more kids are viewed as a major threat to adult society, although different groups—depending on their class, race, gender, and ethnicity—engender different responses. Innocence is not only race specific, it is also gendered. Central to the romantic notion of childhood innocence is the stay-at-home mom, more recently buttressed by the conservative emphasis on family values. As public life is once again separated from the domestic sphere, and as the role of women is limited to an idealized notion of maternity, the requirements of motherhood become the defining principle maintaining the notion of childhood innocence. The myth of childhood innocence infantilizes both women and children while it simultaneously reproduces an extreme imbalance of power between adults and children, on one hand, and men and women, on the other.

The growing assault on youth is evident not only in the withdrawal of government-supported services, once created with their interests in mind, but also in the indignities youth suffer on a daily basis. For example, in schools kids are increasingly subjected to random strip searches, placed under constant electronic surveillance, and forced to submit to random drug testing. Young people are denied dignity and agency, and not just in urban schools. The renaissance of surveillance, control, and regulation in light of the school shootings has resulted in increased calls to place armed security personnel and metal detectors in affluent suburban schools. In what at any other time would have been perceived as an extreme reaction, in the post-Littleton climate, the Dallas-based National Center for Policy Analysis issued a statement calling for the arming of public school teachers; the media characterized this as a legitimate intervention.[21]

The erosion of student civil rights is often coupled with policies that eliminate recess and sports programs, especially in those schools short of financial resources and supplies—schools largely inhabited by poor, working-class kids. At the same time, young people are increasingly excluded from public spaces outside of schools that once offered them the opportunity to hang out with relative security, work with mentors, and develop their own talents and sense of self-worth. Like the concept of citizenship itself, recreational space is now privatized as a commercial profit-making venture. Gone are the youth centers, city public parks, outdoor basketball courts, or empty lots where kids could play stick ball. Play areas are now rented out to the highest bidder, "caged in by steel fences, wrought iron gates, padlocks and razor ribbon wire."[22]

As public space shrivels up, new services arise in the private sector to take "care" of kids. As sociologist Mike Males insightfully argues in his book *Framing Youth* these new "kid-fixing" services take on ominous consequences for many young people:

> Beginning in the mid-1970s, kid-fixing services erupted to meet the market. They were of two kinds. Prison gates opened wide in the 1980s to receive tens of thousands more poorer teens, three-fourths of them non-white. Confinement of minority youths in prisons increased by 80 percent in the last decade. . . . At the same time, mental health and other treatment centers raked in huge profits therapizing hundreds of thousands more health-insured children. . . . Youth treatment is now a $25 billion dollar per year business with a "record of steady profit growth."[23]

Young people often bear the burden of new, undeserved responsibilities and pressures to "grow up." At the same time, their freedoms are curtailed and their constitutional protections and rights of citizenship are restricted. Where can children find narratives of hope, semiautonomous cultural spheres, discussions of meaningful differences, and non market-based democratic identities?[24]

Although adult caretakers and a number of social commentators recognize the new burdens placed on young people and voice concerns about the ways in which childhood is changing, their worries are often defined through highly selective discourses that are closely tied to the class and race of the kids under discussion. For example, liberal commentators on children's culture, such as Neil Postman and David Elkind, argue that the line between childhood and adulthood is disappearing due to the widespread influence of popular culture and the changing nature of the family.[25] Postman believes that popular culture, especially television and child-friendly technologies such as VCRs and computer games, have undermined, if not corrupted, childhood innocence. Indeed the high melodrama of adolescent life as captured in television's *Dawson's Creek* and the hip cynicism of *South Park,* in which one unfortunate eight-year-old named Kenny dies violently in every episode, do seem like a far cry from the family drama of the *Brady Bunch* or the innocence of the *Peanuts* cartoon series that raised an earlier white, middle-class generation. Youth's access to every kind of pornography on the Internet and the technologically advanced, hyperreal violence of video game "home entertainment" systems sound similar kinds of alarms for adults raised on an occasionally titillating issue of *National Geographic* and the flash of the pin-ball machine. It seems, however, that Postman mourns not only the loss of childhood innocence but also the loss of Victorian principles of stern, hardworking, white middle-class families unsullied by the postmodern technologies of the visual age. Curiously, Postman's attack on the corrupting influence of popular culture says little about the media's role in presenting an endless stream of misrepresentations about black and poor youth. Nor does Postman analyze corporate culture's exploitation of childhood innocence and its sexual potential. Postman also ignores the way corporate culture positions young people as both the subject and the object of commodification, as objects to buy and be sold in the marketplace.

Postman's nostalgic longing for high or elite culture constitutes a modernist dream pitting the culture of print (with its own legacy of racist and sexist imagery) against a visual age that allegedly promotes self-indulgence and the enervating illiteracy that both morally tarnishes young people and condemns them to a passive and demeaning role in life. Within Postman's binaristic vision, the loss of childhood innocence is directly attributed to the rise of new electronic technologies and the mass appeal of popular culture.

Such a focus conveniently absolves Postman of the need to question the class, gender, and racial coding that structures his view of the American past and of the need to examine how the political dynamics of a changing economic climate—rather than popular culture—result in cutting the funding for public services for young people while simultaneously cutting short their freedoms and future. What Postman ignores is the fact that popular culture is not only a site of enormous contradiction but also a site of negotiation for kids, one of the few places where they can speak for themselves, produce alternative public spheres, and represent their own interests. It is also one of the most important sites for adults to learn how childhood identities are produced, how effective investments are secured, how desires are mobilized, and how learning can be linked to progressive social change. In many ways, Postman's position is symptomatic of the call by many adults and educators after the Columbine murders to censor the Internet, banish violent video games, and restrict online services for young people. Rather than acknowledge that the new electronic technologies allow kids to immerse themselves in profoundly important forms of social communication, produce a range of creative expressions, and exhibit forms of agency that are both pleasurable and empowering, adults profoundly mistrust the new technologies—in the name of protecting childhood innocence.[26] Rarely is there a serious attempt to find out what kind of meanings children bring to these new electronic cultures, how these cultures enhance the agency of children, or what kids are actually doing with the new media technologies.[27]

In his work on adolescence, child psychologist David Elkind blames the loss of childhood innocence on the changing nature of the American family and the shrinking opportunities the American family offers to most children. He cites the increased responsibility children now have to bear with the rise in two-parent working families, divorced parents, and the huge jump in single-parent families. Elkind also waxes nostalgic for a bygone era that afforded kids greater opportunities to develop their own games, cultures, and adolescent activities. For Elkind, the rise of the middle-class "superkid" is a classic example of children being asked to perform the same tasks their parents do in the outside world—a world marked by shrinking resources, increased competition, and an inflated Horatio Alger notion of achievement.[28]

Both critiques of contemporary youth culture construct childhood innocence as nostalgic, white, middle-class, static, and passive. Children in these discussions are denied agency and live in dire need of protection from the adult world. As such, youth seem to live outside of the political sphere, with all of the implications such a distanced terrain carries for viewing childhood within rather than removed from the varied social, cultural, and economic forces that constitute adult society. But more important, this selective notion of innocence has almost nothing to say about a generation of poor and black youth who do not have the privilege of defining their problems in such narrow terms and for whom the shrinking boundaries between childhood and adulthood dangerously threaten their lives and well-being. For example, as the war against youth escalates, politicians such as Jim Pittis, a Republican legislator from Texas, have attempted to pass state laws that would apply the death penalty to children as young as eleven. Such laws are aimed at poor kids who live in a world in which their most serious problem is certainly not completing excessive loads of homework. On the contrary, these kids live with the daily fear of being incarcerated and the ongoing problems of not having enough food to eat, proper housing, or medical care. Shut out from most state-sponsored social supports and public spaces, Latino and black youth bear the burden of an adult society that either views them as disposable and as a threat to middle-class life, or reifies them through a commercial logic in search of a new market niche.

As the eighteenth century's romantic notion of childhood loses its prominence, childhood is being reinvented, in part through the interests of corporate capital. The myth of the innocent child as an "object of adoration has turned all too easily into the concept of the child as object, and then into marketing of the child as a commodity."[29] Capital has proven powerful enough both to renegotiate what it means to be a child and to make innocence a commercial and sexual category. In this way, the force of capital weakens or counteracts child labor laws and educational entitlements for children.

CORPORATE CULTURE AND THE APPROPRIATION OF INNOCENCE

> It is time to recognize that the true tutors of our children are not schoolteachers or university professors but filmmakers, advertising executives and pop culture purveyors. Disney does more than Duke, Spielberg outweighs Stanford, MTV trumps MIT.
>
> —Benjamin R. Barber, "More Democracy! More Revolution!"

The ascendancy of corporate culture also has created conditions in which adults can exhibit what a writer for *The Nation*, Annette Fuentes, calls a "sour, almost hateful view of young people."[30] For example, a 1997 Public Agenda report, "Kids These Days: What Americans Really Think About the Next Generation," echoes adults' growing fears of and disdain for young people.[31] The report found that two-thirds of the adults surveyed thought that kids today were rude, irresponsible, and wild. Another 58 percent thought that young people will make the world either a worse place or no better when they become adults. Unfortunately, such views are not limited to the findings of conservative research institutes. Former Senator Bill Bradley (D-NJ), a prominent liberal spokesperson, reinforces the ongoing demonization of youth by claiming that the United States is "in danger of losing a generation of young people to a self-indulgent, self-destructive lifestyle."[32] None of these positions call attention to what MIT professor Henry Jenkins calls "the power dynamic between children and adults."[33]

When adults invoke the myth of "childhood innocence" to describe the vulnerability of middle-class kids, they mention child molestation, pedophilia, and the sexual dangers of the Internet as the central threats.[34] This type of discussion assumes that the threat to middle-class kids comes from outside the social formations they inhabit, from forces beyond their control. I do not mean to suggest that pedophiles and abductors are not real menaces (although the danger they pose is ridiculously exaggerated); I merely want to suggest that the image of the pedophile becomes a convenient excuse for ignoring the role that middle-class values and institutional forms actually play in threatening the health and welfare of all children.

This perceived threat to childhood innocence ignores the contradiction between adult concern for the safety of children and the reality of how adults treat children on a daily basis. Most of the violence waged against children is by adults; this includes the 2,000 to 3,000 kids, many of whom are middle class, who are murdered annually by family members and friends. Moreover, too little is said about both a corporate culture that makes a constant spectacle of children's bodies and the motives of specific industries that have a major stake in promoting such exhibitions. Art historian Ann Higonnet touches on this issue in arguing that "The sexualization of children is not a fringe phenomenon inflicted by perverts on a protesting society, but a fundamental change furthered by legitimate industries and millions of satisfied consumers."[35]

The point here is not that millennial corporate culture is interested only in commodifying or sexualizing children; rather it is to underscore the influence corporate culture now wields in redefining the terms through which children's experiences and identities are named, understood, and negotiated. Of course, industries also have audiences, but corporate culture's promotion of the sexualization of children as an advertising gimmick to satisfy consumers and shareholders alike has eroded the distinction between childhood and adulthood.

When it is recognized in the public consciousness that children are not entirely passive and immune and can actually imitate adult behavior, the images of working-class, Latino, and black kids are invoked as a media spectacle. Their aberrant behavior is invariably attributed to the irresponsibilities of working mothers, rampant drug abuse, and other alleged corruptions of morality circulating within working-class culture. But little is mentioned about the violence perpetrated by those middle-class values and social formations—such as conspicuous consumption, conformity, snobbery, and ostracism—that reproduce racial, class, and gender exclusions. Nor is much said about how middle-class values legitimate and regulate the cultural hierarchies that demean marginalized groups and reinforce racial and economic inequalities. Rather than confront the limitations and bias of middle-class values, conservatives battle against the welfare state, dismantle many important child-service programs, and promote economic policies and mergers that facilitate corporate downsizing—without facing much resistance from the Democratic party. Moreover, the national media rarely acknowledges or criticizes those forces within American culture that chip away at the notion of education as a public good or the disastrous effects conservative educational policy might have for working-class families and their children.

Similarly, dominant media invokes popular culture, but not the corporations that produce and regulate it, as a threat to children's purity. Consider the following contradictions. Pornography on the Internet is held up as an immanent danger to childhood innocence, but nothing is said about the corporations and their middle-class shareholders who relentlessly commodify and sexualize children's bodies, desires, and identities in the interest of turning a profit. Mainstream media critics who focus on the disappearance of childhood endlessly argue that the greatest threat to childhood innocence comes from rap music rather than from media conglomerates such as Time-Warner (which produces many rap artists), General Electric, Westinghouse, or Disney.[36] Corporate culture's appropriation of childhood innocence and purity is rarely fodder for serious discussion, while corporations such as Calvin Klein trade on the appeal of childhood innocence by exploiting its sexual potential in order to sell cologne, underwear, and jeans. Slick, high-end fashion magazines offer up Lolita-like fourteen-year-olds as the newest supermodels and sex symbols, while Madonna appears in a 1992 photo spread for *Vanity Fair* with her hair in pigtails, her makeup sultry, a blatant erotic baby-woman.[37] In these instances of corporate hustling, the emotional resonance of childhood innocence becomes erotically charged as it is recontextualized within the commercial sphere. Many critics view such images as further proof that children are under assault. They are less concerned about the ever expanding reach of corporate culture into every facet of children's culture than they are alarmed by the growing sexualization of popular culture, with its celebration of the "smut" produced by gangsta rap (and its seeming vindication of a sexually charged music/video industry) and its potential to incite the ever-looming presence of the pedophile.

But the images that create such uneasiness are not limited to the perceived looming threat to dominant culture from pedophiles and rap artists. On the contrary, the threat to innocence and childhood takes many forms. Commercial culture has removed childhood from the civic discussion of rights, public responsibility, and equality and turned it into a commodity. For example, in an endless array of mass media advertisements, innocence is reduced to an aesthetic or a psychological trope that prompts adults to find their "inner child," adopt teen fashions, and buy a range of services designed to make them look younger. This type of adult infantilization enables them to identify with youth while it simultaneously empties adulthood of its political, economic, and social responsibilities and educative functions. Too many adults rely on the commercial language of self-help and character formation to further their own self-obsession while ignoring the social problems they create for kids, especially for those who are disadvantaged by virtue of their class, gender, or race. Such indifference allows adults to impose on young people the demands and responsibilities they themselves have abandoned.

Childhood at the end of the twentieth century is not ending as a historical and social category; it has simply been transformed into a market strategy and a fashion aesthetic used to expand the consumer-based needs of privileged adults who live within a market culture that has little concern for ethical considerations, noncommercial spaces, or public responsibilities."Childhood innocence no longer inspires adults to fight for the rights of children, enact reforms that invest in their future, or provide them with "the tools to realize their own political agendas or to participate in the production of their own culture."[38] On the contrary, as culture becomes increasingly commercialized, the only type of citizenship that adult society offers to children is that of consumerism.

At the same time, children are expected to act like adults, although different demands are made on different groups of kids. Children, asked to shoulder enormous responsibilities, often respond by mimicking and emulating adult behaviors, which they are then condemned for appropriating. Of course, when privileged white kids mimic destructive adult behavior, such acts are generally treated as aberrations. But when disadvantaged kids do so, it becomes a social problem for which they are both the root cause and the victims. At the same time, young people who refuse to imitate adults' own social and political indifference and actually take on a number of important social issues and responsibilities are usually marginalized or ignored.[39]

Recent commentaries on contemporary youth largely miss the fact that what is changing, if not disappearing, are productive social bonds between adults and children. Today's embattled concept of childhood magnifies how adult society acts upon an ethically stripped-down notion of social responsibility, especially as it pertains to how adults define their relationships to young people. This becomes evident in the ways childhood is increasingly being marketed, in the move away from making social investments in children, and in the stepped-up efforts to disempower and contain them.

Current representations of youth—which range from depicting kids as a threat to society or as defenseless against the corrupting

influence of the all-powerful popular culture—often work to undermine any productive sense of agency among young people, offering
few possibilities for analyzing how children actually experience and
mediate relationships with each other or with adults. In the post-
Littleton climate, moral panic and fear replace critical understanding and allow media pundits such as Barbara Kantrowitz and Pat
Wingert to proclaim in a *Newsweek* article that white suburban
youth have a dark side and that youth culture in general represents
"*Lord of the Flies* on a vast scale."[40] Such representations not only
diminish the complexity of children's lives; they also erase any
understanding of how power relations between adults and young
people work against many children. At the same time, the discourse
of hope is replaced with the rhetoric of cynicism and disdain.

As the current assault on youth grows more expansive, extending beyond the inner city, it is accompanied by numerous films,
books, and media representations that focus on youth culture in a
way that would have appeared socially irresponsible twenty years
ago. Films such as *Jawbreaker, Varsity Blues, Ten Things I Hate About
You*, and *Cruel Intentions* relentlessly celebrate mindless, testoster-
one-driven, infantilized males at the top of a repressive school
pecking order or equally vacuous, but also ruthless, arrogant,
sexually manipulative girls, who come dangerously close to being
cold-blooded psychopaths. Films such as *Election* resonate powerfully with the broader public that views a growing number of white
suburban kids as inane, neurotically self-centered, or sexually
deviant. These films reinforce the assumption that such kids are in
need of medical treatment, strict controls, or disciplinary supervi-
sion. Moreover, these attacks complement and further legitimate
the racist backlash against minority youth that has gained prominence in American society in the last decade of the twentieth
century.[41] In popular culture, this backlash can be seen in Hollywood films such as *The Substitute, Kids,* and *187,* which are premised
on the assumption that brown, black, and poor kids are not simply
a threat but a menace to a white, middle-class notion of childhood

innocence and society because they embody criminality, corruption, rampant sexuality, and moral degeneracy. In these films, youth are not only demonized but also marked as disposable, literally murdered as part of a "cleaning-up" operation to make the public schools and urban streets safe for a largely white, middle-class adult population whose well-being and security are allegedly under siege.

As the line between childhood and adulthood is renegotiated, the notion of childhood innocence serves as a historical and social referent for understanding that the current moral panic over youth is primarily about the crisis of democratic society itself and its waning ability to offer children the social, cultural, and economic opportunities and resources they need to both survive and prosper in this society.

In such a perverse climate, innocence represents more than fertile ground for a media machine that increasingly legitimates the cultural face of corporate power. The myth of innocence is also the rhetoric of choice of politicians and academics who rely on it to bash single mothers, gay and lesbian families, the legacy of the 1960s, popular culture, and kids themselves.

Public concerns about the loss of childhood innocence do at times consider youth as a valuable resource that needs to be nurtured and protected; more frequently, however, the rhetoric of innocence displaces this important sense of adult responsibility and views innocence as quite exclusionary. In so doing a line is drawn between those kids worthy of adult protection and those who appear beyond the pale of adult compassion and concern. Yet, increasingly, those kids who fall under the mantle of adult protection suffer a loss of agency in the name of being sheltered by adult authority. Innocence in this perspective has little to do with empowering youth, with prompting adults to be more self-critical about how they wield power over young people, or with offering young people supportive environments where they can produce their own cultural experiences. Innocence has a politics, one defined less by a recognition of the need for adults to invest in the welfare of youth or to recognize their remarkable achievements than by the widening gap between the public's professed concern about the fate of young people and the deteriorating conditions under which many live. The deteriorating state of America's children can be seen in the increased number of children living in poverty—20.5 percent of all children; the large number of children without affordable housing—more than 6.8 million; as well as in the large number of American children who lack health insurance. According to a 1998 study by the *Children's Defense Report* all of these figures have increased since 1996. Not only are there twenty million children living in poverty in the United States, but the United States ranks in the lower half of Western industrialized countries in providing family support services.

When viewed from outside the logic of the market, even the terms of the debate about children seem to rest on deception. For many commentators and politicians who loudly proclaim that innocence is under assault, the welfare of children is not really at stake. Rather, they mourn a mythical view of nationhood, citizenship, and community that is largely projected onto another time and place when white middle-class values were protected from the evils of popular culture, the changing nature of the workforce, and the rise of immigration. This narrative provides nothing less than a biblical account of childhood innocence and its fall in which youth appears as a universalized category, history seems removed from the taint of contradictory forces, and adult society takes on the nostalgic glow of an Andrew Wyeth painting.

This nostalgic discourse often betrays bad faith on the part of adults purportedly acting in the interest of young people, as was amply displayed in the post-Littleton controversy over youth, school violence, and popular culture. For example, House Majority Leader Tom DeLay (R-Texas), shamelessly using the tragedy to further his own conservative political agenda, appeared on Fox News television and argued that one response to the school massacre would be to put God back into the schools. Former

Secretary of Education William Bennett railed against a popular youth fad known as Goth culture (a subculture that embraces black clothing, industrial music, pale make-up, and black lipstick) and used the Littleton tragedy as a platform to denigrate popular culture, reinforcing the notion that kids who are "different" deserve to be scorned and ridiculed. He seemed to forget that many Littleton students felt that just such scorn and ridicule contributed to the hostile school environment that exacerbated the killers' pent-up rage. Neither DeLay nor Bennett had much to say about how such attacks further exclude youth nor did they provide ample testimony revealing that adults in general have little interest in listening to kids' problems in school or to how they construct their experiences outside of traditional societal values. Nor do most adults pay attention to how the culture of the Internet, video games, industrial rock, computerized gladiator matches, and androgynous fashions provide an important resource for kids to develop their own cultural identities and sense of social agency. And neither DeLay nor Bennett had much to say about passing legislation that would eliminate widespread poverty among children, eradicate children's access to guns, and reverse the mounting expense of building more and more prisons. All three of these troubling issues limit educational and work opportunities for many young people, especially those from the underclasses. There is more at stake here than the critical vocabulary used to understand how youth are shaped within the current social order; commentators also refuse to discuss how the basic institutions of adult society increasingly participate in a culture of violence that cares more about profits than human needs and the public good. While adult society is obsessed with youth, it refuses to deal with what it means to uphold youth, to invest in their well-being, and to offer them the opportunities to become successful adults.

Commentators such as sociologist Mike Males argue that the late 1990s represent "the most anti-youth period in American history."[42] James Wagoner, the president of the social service organization Advocates for Youth, claims that "Young people have been portrayed almost universally as a set of problems to be managed by society: juvenile crime, teen-age pregnancy, drug use."[43] Both men suggest that American society has undergone a profound change in the last two decades, in terms of how it views youth and in how it treats them.[44] Underlying this shift are a number of social problems that are rarely discussed or critically analyzed, such as racism, poverty, unemployment, and the dismantling of child care services. While many adults appear consumed with young people, they are not concerned with listening to their needs or addressing their problems. How our society treats its youth, and how it balances corporate needs and democratic values, can be seen in the contraditction between the rhetoric of childhood innocence and the reality of despair and suffering that many children face daily.

In what follows, I want to highlight the relationship between the ongoing assault on youth and the responsibility of educators to address this crisis. In doing so, I emphasize the need for educators to connect their work to the political task of making research, teaching, and learning part of the dynamic of democratic change itself.

PUBLIC PEDAGOGY AND THE RESPONSIBILITY OF INTELLECTUALS

> What do we represent? Whom do we represent? Are we responsible? For what and to whom? If there is a university responsibility, it at least begins with the moment when a need to hear these questions, to take them upon oneself and respond, is imposed. This imperative for responding is the initial form and minimal requirement of responsibility.
>
> —Jacques Derrida, "Mochlos; or the Conflict of the Faculties"

The last few decades have been a time of general crisis in university life. Issues regarding the meaning and purpose of higher education, the changing nature of what counts as knowledge in a multicultural society, growing dissent among underpaid adjunct faculty and graduate assistants, the increasing vocationalization of university life—with its emphasis on learning corporate skills—battles over affirmative action, and intensifying struggles over the place of politics in teaching have exacerbated the traditional tensions both within the university community and between the university and the broader society. As the quotation above indicates, Jacques Derrida, the French philosopher, raises timely fundamental questions not only for university teachers but for all educators and parents. In response to the ongoing crisis in the university, I have tried to consider fundamental links between knowledge and power, teaching practices and effects, authority and civic responsibility. I have argued elsewhere that the question of what educators teach is inseparable from what it means to invest in public life, to locate oneself and one's students in a public dialogue. Implicit in this argument is the assumption that the educators' responsibilities cannot be separated from the consequences of the knowledge they produce, the social relations they legitimate, and the ideologies they disseminate.[45] At its best, educational work responds to the questions and issues posed by the tensions and contradictions of public life and attempts to understand and intervene in specific problems that emanate from the material contexts of everyday existence.

Educational work is both inseparable from and a participant in cultural politics because it is in the realm of culture that identities are forged, citizenship rights are enacted, and possibilities are developed for translating acts of interpretation into forms of intervention. "Pedagogy" in this discourse is about linking the construction of knowledge to issues of ethics, politics, and power. Making the political more pedagogical requires that educators address how agency unfolds within power-infused relations; that is, how the very processes of learning constitute the political mechanisms through which identities are produced, desires are mobilized, and experiences take on specific forms and meanings. This broad definition of pedagogy is not limited to what goes on in institutionalized forms of schooling; it encompasses every relationship youth imagine to be theirs in the world. So to understand and overcome today's assault on youth, educators need to rethink the interrelated dynamics of politics, culture, power, and responsibility and redefine their own political role.

Educators and other adults need to recognize that the political, economic, and social forces that demonize young people and reduce funding to the public services youth rely on also affect public schools and universities. The increasing influence of corporate power in commercializing youth and eliminating the noncommercial spheres where youth meet and develop a sense of agency and autonomy is certainly related to corporate culture's attempts to turn institutions of public and higher education over to the imperatives of the market. Moreover, the continued devaluation of education as a public good points to the need for educators to work together to reclaim schools as democratic public spheres. Crucial to such a struggle is the recognition that the act of reclamation cannot be removed from broader economic, cultural, and social struggles that affect the lives of many young people. I am not suggesting that educators should separate the academic and the political, the performance of institutional politics from cultural politics; rather they must find ways to connect the politics of schooling with political struggles that take place across multiple social spheres and institutions.[46] In this context, cultural politics constructs itself in response to the demands of both the institutional contexts of schooling—in all of their differences—and the broader demands and practical commitments that point to change and resistance in ideological and institutional structures that oppress young people daily.

Cultural politics challenges corporate culture's exclusive emphasis on the private good and reconnects educational theory and criticism to a notion of the public good that links democracy in culture with democracy in the wider domain of public history and ordinary life. Broadly defined, culture in this perspective breaks down the divide between elite and popular culture and extends the reach of what counts as a serious object of learning from the library and the museum to mass media and popular culture. Similarly, the politics of culture not only reconstitutes and maps how meaning is produced, it also investigates the connections between discourses and structures of material power, the production of knowledge and the effects it has when translated into daily life. But before educators can rethink what it means to make connections to popular formations beyond the walls of formal educational institutions, they will have to analyze the force of the institutional and ideological structures that shape their own lives.

Critical educators need to address what it means to exercise authority from their own academic locations and experiences while assuming the challenge of putting knowledge in the service of a more realized democracy. Doing this requires redefining the relationship between theory and practice in order to challenge theory's formalist legacy, one that often abstracts it from concrete problems and the dynamics of power. Theory in this sense is reduced to a form of theoreticism, an indulgence in which the production of theoretical discourse becomes an end in itself, a mere expression of language removed from the possibility of challenging strategies of domination. Rather than bridging the gap between public practices and intellectual debates or implementing political projects that merge strategies of understanding and social engagement, theory often becomes an end for professional advancement. Cut off from concrete struggles and broader public debates, theory often emphasizes rhetorical mastery and cleverness rather than the politically responsible task of challenging the inertia of commonsense understandings of the world, opening up possibilities for new approaches to social reform, or addressing the most pressing social problems that young people have to face.

Similarly, in many liberal and critical approaches to education, the politics of meaning is relevant only to the degree that it is separated from a broader politics of engagement. Reading texts is removed from larger social and political contexts, and engages questions of power exclusively within a politics of representation. Such readings largely function to celebrate a textuality that has been diminished to a bloodless formalism, and the nonthreatening, if not accommodating, affirmation of indeterminacy as a transgressive aesthetic. Lost here is any semblance of a radical political project that as George Lipsitz points out "grounds itself in the study of concrete cultural practices and . . . understands that struggles over meaning are inevitably struggles over resources."[47] By failing to connect the study of texts to the interests of expanding the goals of economic justice, children's rights campaigns, radical democratic visions, and opposition to antiwelfare and immigration policies, many educators conceive of politics as largely representational or abstractly theoretical.[48] They also miss the crucial opportunity to develop connections between analyses of representations and strategies of political engagement, that is, they fail to use critical readings of texts as "routes to a larger analysis of historical formations."[49]

To address the problems of youth, rigorous educational work needs to respond to the dilemmas of the outside world by focusing on how young people make sense of their possibilities for agency within the power-regulated relations of everyday life. The motivation for scholarly work cannot be narrowly academic; such work must connect with "real life social and political issues in the wider society."[50] This requires, in part, that educators address the practical consequences of their work in the broader society while simultaneously making connections to those too-often-ignored institutional forms and cultural spheres that position and influence young people within unequal relations of power. Moreover, critical educators must recognize that the forms of domination that bear down on young people are both institutional and cultural, and one cannot be separated from the other. Within this approach, the effects of domination cannot be removed from the educational conditions in which such behavior is learned, appropriated, or challenged.

Analyzing the relationship between culture and politics also requires that critical educators engage the symbolic and the material conditions that construct the various social formations in which young people experience themselves and their relations to others. That is, any viable form of cultural politics must address the institutional machineries of power that promote child poverty, violence, unemployment, police brutality, rape, sexual abuse, and racism. But this is not enough. Educators also must question those cultural pedagogies that produce specific meanings, affective investments, and desires that legitimate and secure acts of domination aimed at young people. Educators must do more than simply interview youth through academic-based research methods. They must become border crossers (without passports), willing to examine the multiple sites and cultural forms that young people produce in order to make their voices heard within the larger society. Ann Powers, a writer for the New York Times, has insightfully pointed out that as young people have been shut out of the larger society, they have created their own web sites, alternative radio programs, "published their own manifestoes in photocopied fanzines, made their own music and shared it on cassette, designed their own fashions and arranged to have them sold in boutiques."[51] Moreover, Powers has argued that many young women have not sat passively by as they see themselves misrepresented in the American cultural landscape as lazy, shiftless, dangerous, and pathological. In response, they have produced a "far-ranging girls' culture, which includes bold young athletes, musicians, film makers and writers [which] is invigorating the discourse of women's liberation. [In addition], activist groups like YELL, an ACT Up youth division . . . have devised new approaches to safe sex education."[52] Today's diverse youth culture suggests that educators and adults become more attentive to the cultural formations that young people inhabit while making a serious effort to read, listen, and learn from the languages, social relations, and many types of symbolic expression that young people produce.

Cultural theorist Jon Katz convincingly argues that "children are at the epicenter of the information revolution, ground zero of the digital world. They helped build it, they understand it as well as, or better than anyone else [and] they occupy a new kind of cultural space."[53] This is a particularly important insight in light of the attacks on the media and the call for censoring the Internet that arose after the Littleton massacre. These technological sites produce public pedagogies and must be engaged seriously as knowledge-producing technologies and spheres that demand new types of learning and critical skills from both young people and adults. Many educators and adults need to redefine their own understanding of the new technologies and the new literacies they have produced. The new media, including the Internet and computer culture, need to become serious objects of educational analysis and learning, especially in the elementary and public schools. The social affiliations, groups, and cultural experiences these media establish must be legitimated and incorporated into the school curricula as seriously as the study of history, English, and language arts. Students need to have opportunities, as Henry Jenkins points out, to form supportive communities around their interest in and use of digital media, just as the schools need to make media literacy and media production central to the learning process for young people.[54]

But if educators, adults, and others are to take seriously what it means to link academic criticism to public knowledge and strategies of intervention, they will have to reevaluate the relationship between culture and power as a starting point. Doing this requires becoming more attentive to how politics is worked out in urban spaces and cultural formations that are currently experiencing the full force of the attack on youth. Critical educators must give meaning to the belief that academic work matters in relation to broader public practices and policies. In part, this suggests that educators address what critical theorist Cornel West has called the crisis of vision and meaning that currently characterizes all levels of schooling and culture in the United States. The crisis of vision reflects the political, social, and cultural demise of democratic relations and values in American institutions and culture. Due to the pervasive despair among and possibility of resistance from youth, educators must link educational work, both within and outside of schools, to "what it means to expand the scope of democracy and democratic institutions, [and to] address [how] the very conditions of democracy are being undermined."[55] Such work may lead to an understanding not just of how power operates in particular contexts but also how the knowledge and skills produced and learned within diverse locations "will better enable people to change the contexts and hence the relations of power."[56] Such relations of power inform the inequalities that undermine democratic participation in a wide variety of cultural spheres, including public and higher education.

In the post-Littleton climate, the crisis of vision provides an opportunity for adults, parents, and others to organize and address the crisis of meaning that permeates late-capitalist societies. This crisis is embodied in the growing ascendancy of corporate power, the shrinking of noncommercialized public spaces, and the spread of market values that has undermined those elements of care, respect, and compassion for others that are central to any decent, democratic society. Cornel West rightly argues that the usurpation of democratic values by market values has resulted in a "creeping zeitgeist of cold-heartedness and mean-spiritedness" that he terms the "gangsterization of American culture."[57] Any viable form of cultural politics needs to recognize how the "gangsterization of American culture" reproduces and reinforces the crisis of vision and meaning for many Americans, especially young people, who are struggling to redefine their identities within a set of relations based on notions of solidarity, justice, service, and conviction—values that seem totally marginal to their daily lives and the institutions that bear down on them. The challenge of children's culture cannot be abstracted from the political, economic, and social crisis of democracy itself. This challenge needs to reinvigorate the relationship between theoretical work and practical struggles, between cultural politics and the struggle to change institutional machineries of power. Progressive educators should question the purpose and meaning of their social function and critically address their responsibilities for educating students, adults, and others to fulfill their obligations as critical and engaged citizens. Central to such a challenge is the need to develop a language of social justice that is part of a broader understanding of what it means to be educated and what is involved in educating within a variety of cultural and social contexts.

FORECAST

The first section of this book examines a variety of cultural contexts in which many adults, in spite of the public concern over the notion of childhood, fail to provide both a measure of nurturing and the necessary conditions for young people to negotiate and challenge the dominant social forms that shape their lives. More specifically, I explore how childhood innocence is appropriated within and across dominant cultural forms such as the child beauty pageant, the fashion industry, and the commercialization of public schools. I then analyze the contradictions and the implications these cultural forms have for children's lives and well-being, especially for those youth who are marginalized by virtue of gender, class, and race.

In the second section of the book, I examine the current assault on youth and argue that in order to address this crisis, educators need to develop a new language that emphasizes the substantive role of culture not only in the formation of dominant social structures and unequal power relations but also as an area of struggle over institutional contexts, meanings, and identities. In analyzing the work of theorists such as Antonio Gramsci, Paulo Freire, and Stuart Hall, I examine the need for critical dialogues that discuss the importance of linking culture, politics, and context through the development of a public pedagogy in which theory responds to the problems posed within particular contexts. I use the work of Gramsci, Freire, and Hall to illustrate the educational and performative nature of culture as a pedagogical and political practice. I also draw on their work to demonstrate culture's value in developing a democratic politics that addresses the relations of power between youth and adults.

Connecting the two sections of the book is the assumption that politics, if it is to be taken up educationally and performatively, must begin by using the best theoretical resources available to change the contexts and relations of power that structure young people's lives. At best, this suggests that politics becomes practical by acknowledging the need to develop projects that emerge out of particular social formations, places, and practices. Central to such a project is the need to begin where young people actually live their lives. Hence, the first section of the book begins not with abstract theoretical formulations but with very specific contexts, sites, and spaces in which youth are both the subject and the object of adult desires, ideologies, and relations of power. Theory is used to explore these contexts and to fashion new imagined possibilities in order to bear witness to the ethical and political dilemmas that animate such contexts and their connection to the larger social landscape. Implicit in this approach is a notion of cultural politics that highlights how education might be used to engage the tension between existing social practices and the moral imperatives of a radical democratic society.

Also connecting both sections of the book is the assumption that, in order to become critical, pedagogy must become performative. Section I focuses on the broad educational force of teaching in shaping everyday experience, understood as a lived appropriation of knowledge, desire, meaning, and values—although not always an object critically analyzed by those who are shaped by it. In section II pedagogy represents a particular form of theorizing that is also critical and action-oriented because it provides a theoretical space for examining the commonsense assumptions, practices, and contradictions that shape daily life.

Both sections acknowledge what it means to live in a world that has been radically altered by corporations and new electronic technologies. Each also addresses how new modes of symbolic and social practice change the way we think about power, social agency, and youth, and what such changes mean for expanding and deepening the process of democratic education, social relations, and public life.

Throughout this book cultural politics is addressed as a particular practice and way of thinking. It is derived from the relationship between texts and contexts, meaning and institutional power, critical reflection and informed action. That is, it provides theoretical tools for considering how knowledge and power can be analyzed within particular spaces and places. Such analysis is especially crucial when such contexts frame the intersection of language and bodies as they become "part of the process of forming and disrupting power relations."[58] At the same time, cultural politics offers an opportunity for parents, educators, and others to better understand how public discussions of youth have been transformed into discourses of control, surveillance, and demonization. Questioning how power works through language practices and institutional formations offers progressives the opportunity to challenge the endless stereotypes and myths that legitimate repressive legislative policies that serve to contain youth and undermine much needed social investments in their future.

Such an approach cannot consist of a series of empty appeals to innocence or the ritualistic condemnation of young people; rather, critical attention must be paid to the historical, social, and institutional conditions that produce those structures of power and ideology that bear down on youth in their everyday existence.

SECTION I

CORPORATE POWER AND THE CULTURE OF EVERYDAY LIFE

ONE

Nymphet Fantasies: Child Beauty Pageants and the Politics of Innocence

Only in a climate of denial could hysteria over satanic rituals at daycare centers coexist with a failure to grasp the full extent of child abuse. (More than 8.5 million women and men are survivors.) Only in a culture that represses the evidence of the senses could child pageantry grow into a $5 billion dollar industry without anyone noticing. Only in a nation of promiscuous puritans could it be a good career move to equip a six-year-old with bedroom eyes.

—Richard Goldstein, *Village Voice*, June 24, 199

THE DISAPPEARING CHILD AND THE POLITICS OF INNOCENCE

The notion of the disappearing child and the myth of childhood innocence often mirror and support each other. Within the myth of innocence, children are often portrayed as inhabiting a world that is untainted, magical, and utterly protected from the harshness of adult life. In this scenario, innocence not only erases the complexities of childhood and the range of experiences different children encounter, but it also offers an excuse for adults to evade responsibility for how children are firmly connected to and shaped by the social and cultural institutions run largely by adults. Innocence in this instance makes children invisible except as projections of adult fantasies—fantasies that allow adults to believe that children do not suffer from their greed, recklessness, perversions of will and spirit and that adults are, in the final analysis, unaccountable for their actions.[1]

If innocence provides the moral ethos that distinguishes children from adults, the discourse that deals with the disappearance of childhood in our culture signals that it is being threatened by forces that tend to collapse that distinction. For example, in cultural critic Neil Postman's thoroughly modernist view of the world, the electronic media, especially television, presents a threat to the existence of children and the civilized culture bequeathed to the West by the Enlightenment.[2] Not only does the very character of television—its fast-paced format, sound-byte worldview, information overload, and narrative organization—undermine the very possibility for children to engage in critical thinking, but its content works to expel images of the child from its programming by both "adultifying" the child and promoting the rise of the "childfied" adult.[3] But Postman is quick to extend his thesis to other spheres, noting, for example, the disappearance of children's clothing and children's games, the entry of children into professional sports, and the increasing willingness of the criminal justice system to treat children as miniature adults. Postman's lament represents less a concern with preserving childhood innocence than a cry for the passing of a world in which popular culture threatens high culture, and the culture of print loses its hold on a restricted and dominant notion of literacy and citizenship training. The loss of childhood innocence in this scenario marks the passing of a historical and political time in which children could be contained and socialized under the watchful tutelage of such dominant regulatory institutions as the family, school, and church.

Many politicians eager to establish themselves as protectors of childhood innocence also have appropriated the specter of the child as an endangered species. In their rush to implement new social and economic policies, numerous politicians hold up children as both the inspiration for and prime beneficiaries of their reforms. Lacking opportunities to vote, mobilize, or register their opinions, young children become an easy target and referent in discussions of moral uplift and social legitimation. They also become pawns and victims. Far from benefiting children, many of the programs and government reforms enacted in the late 1990s by Clinton and the Republican-led Congress represent what Senator Edward Kennedy (D-MA) has called "legislative child abuse."[4] Protecting the innocence of children appears to have a direct connection with the disappearing child, although not in the sense predicted by Neil Postman. The draconian cuts in welfare reform enacted in the 1996 Personal Responsibility and Work Opportunity Reconciliation Act are having a devastating effect on a great number of poor families and their children. While welfare roles have declined since 1996, a report released by the National Conference of State Legislatures indicated that 40 to 60 percent of the poor people who leave welfare obtain employment but often at below-poverty-level wages. Moreover, assistance has been terminated for substantial numbers of children with disabilities. Meanwhile, thousands of families are losing welfare aid because of penalties for noncompliance with new welfare reform rules, and many of those who lose benefits do not find work. Harsh compliance measures, inadequate child care, marginal employment, low wages, and lack of adequate transportation for poor families all combine to make a mockery of welfare reform.[5] In this instance, children are indeed disappearing—right into the hole of poverty, suffering, and despair.[6] In short, the language of innocence suggests a concern for all children but often ignores or disparages the conditions under which many of them are forced to live, especially those who are generally excluded because of race or class from the privileging and protective invocation of innocence.

Politicians have little interest in the welfare of kids who are poor and nonwhite. In view of this fact, innocence emerges less as a term used to highlight the disappearance of kids than as a metaphor for advancing a conservative political agenda based on so-called family values, in which middle-class white children are viewed as more valued and deserving of the material resources and cultural goods of the larger society than are poor and nonwhite children.[7] In this selective appropriation, innocence turns with a vengeance on its humanitarian impulse: The everyday experience of childhood is held hostage to the realities of power and the disingenuous rhetoric of political pragmatism.

As the rhetoric of child welfare heats up in the public consciousness, innocence is increasingly being redeployed by politicians, journalists, and media pundits to rearticulate which specific children are deserving of entitlements and adult protection and what forces pose a threat to them. Imbued with political and ideological values, innocence as used by the popular press is not merely selective about which children are endangered and need to be protected; it also is used to signal who and what constitutes a threat to children.

As politicians, the popular press, and the media increasingly use "the child" as a moral yardstick it becomes more difficult for adults to fail to take responsibility for what they do to kids. Consequently, childhood innocence appears both threatened and threatening. According to popular wisdom, the enemies of children are not to be found in the halls of Congress, in the poisonous advertisements that commodify and sexualize young children, or even in the endless media bashing that blames children for all of society's ills.[8] On the contrary, the child molesters, pedophiles, abductors, and others who prey on children in the most obscene ways imaginable are the biggest threat to children. Here the notion of childhood innocence does more than produce the rhetoric of political opportunism; it also provides the basis for moral panic. Both conservatives and liberals have fed off the frenzy of fear associated with a decade of revelations of alleged child abuse. Starting with the 1987 McMartin preschool case, a wave of fear-inspired legislation has swept the nation to protect children from pedophiles, child molesters, predatory priests and teachers, and anyone else who might be labeled as a sexual deviant who poses a threat to the innocence of children.[9] Child abuse in this scenario is reduced to the individual pathology of the molester and pedophile; the fear and anger it arouses are so great that the Supreme Court is willing to suspend certain constitutional liberties in order to keep sexual predators locked up even after they finish serving their sentences.[10]

But the issue of widespread child abuse has done more than inspire a national fear of child molesters. It points beyond the language of individual pathology to the more threatening issue of how society treats its children, exposing the degree to which children have not been provided with the security and resources necessary to insure their safety and well-being. While the most disturbing threat to innocence may be child abuse, this form of abuse cannot be assessed only through the horrible behavior of sexual predators. Such abuse needs to be situated within a broader set of political, economic, and social considerations; such considerations probe deeply into the cultural formations that not only make children visible markers of humanity and public responsibility but also see them as a menacing enemy or as merely a market to be exploited. The social investment in children's innocence may be at the center of political rhetoric in the halls of Congress, but other forces in American society aggressively breed a hatred and disregard for young people, especially those who are excluded because of their class, race, gender, or status as non-U.S. citizens.

Here I argue that the central threat to childhood innocence lies not in the figure of the pedophile or sexual predator but in the diminishing public spheres available for children to experience themselves as critical agents. Children must be able to develop their capacities for individual and social development free from the debilitating burdens of hunger, poor healthcare, and dilapidated schools, while simultaneously being provided with fundamental social services such as state protection from abusive parents. As cities become increasingly ghettoized because of the ravaging effects of deindustrialization, loss of revenue, and white flight, children are left with fewer educational, social, and economic services to fulfill their needs and desires. As public schools are abandoned or surrendered to the dictates of the market, children increasingly find themselves isolated and removed from the discourses of community and compassion. As the state is hollowed out and only its most brutal apparatuses—police, prisons, etc.—remain intact, children have fewer opportunities to protect themselves from an adult world that offers them dwindling resources, dead-end jobs, and diminished hopes for the future.[11] At the same time, children are increasingly subjected to social and economic forces that exploit them through the dynamics of sexualization, commodification, and commercialization.[12]

JONBENET RAMSEY, RACE, AND THE PERILS OF HOME

While the concept of innocence may incite adults to publicly proclaim their support for future generations, more often than not it protects adults from the reality of society and the negative influence they have in contributing to the ever-increasing impoverishment of children's lives. Of course, flash points in a society often signal that children are in danger and that certain elements in the culture pose a threat to their innocence. Conservatives, for example, have focused on the dangers presented by rap music, cinematic violence, and drugs to launch an attack on Hollywood films, the fashion world, single teen moms, and what it calls the cultural elite. But rarely do conservative and liberal critics focus on the ongoing threats to children at the center of dominant economic, political, and cultural relations—the dismantling of welfare benefits for poor children, particularly cuts in health insurance, food stamps, and housing allowances; the growing assault on young black males through an ever-expanding criminal justice system, and the increasing demonization of young teens in the media.

Poverty, racism, sexism, and the dismantling of the welfare state do great harm to children, but the press does not report most of the stories exemplifying the effects of these social conditions; if it does, little public discussion or self-examination follows.

One recent exception can be found in the case of JonBenet Ramsey, the six-year-old who was found strangled in her wealthy parents' Boulder, Colorado home the day after Christmas in 1996. Throughout the first half of 1997, the press fixated on the case. Major media networks, newspapers, and tabloids besieged the public with photographs and television footage of JonBenet, dubbed the slain little beauty queen, posing coquettishly in a tight dress, wearing bright red lipstick, her hair bleached blond. The case revealed once again that the media gravitate toward victims that fit the dominant culture's image of itself. Not only are children who are white, blond, and middle class invested with more humanity, they become emblematic of a social order that banishes from consciousness any recognition of abused children who "don't fit the image of purity defiled."[13]

Consider the case of a nine-year-old African American child, labeled in the press Girl X. Girl X was raped, beaten, blinded, murdered, and dumped in a stairwell in the rundown Cabrini Green Housing Project in Chicago. The brutal murder aroused a great deal of publicity in Chicago but was virtually ignored by the national media. Race and poverty relegated Girl X to a nonentity. Innocence is applied primarily to children who are white and middle class, often tucked away in urban townhouses and the safe sanctuaries of segregated suburban America. But there is something equally disturbing about the JonBenet Ramsey case. Innocence also masks the sexualization and commodification of young girls who are taught to identify themselves through the pleasures and desires of the adult gaze. The child becomes the principal incitement of adult desire, but the educational and commercial practices at work remain unexamined because they take place within acceptable cultural forms such as children's beauty pageants. This murder also challenges the assumption that privileged families are immune to accusations of child abuse or neglect. The death of the young beauty queen raises serious questions about the cultural practices and institutions of everyday life that shape children's lives, often in ways that undermine children's chances of entering adulthood free from violence, intimidation, and abuse.

I argue that by critically examining the beauty pageant we can begin to see how the language of innocence obscures from the public's view the appropriation, sexualization, and commercialization of children's bodies. In pursuing this argument, I examine how the culture of child beauty pageants functions as a site where young girls learn about pleasure, desire, and the roles they might assume in an adult society. I also examine how such pageants are rationalized, how they are upheld by commercial and ideological structures within the broader society, and how they are reproduced, reinforced, and sustained in related spheres such as advertising and fashion photography—spheres that also play an important role in marketing children as objects of pleasure, desire, and sexuality. Here I attempt to challenge the concept of such rituals as innocent, to reconsider the role they play as part of a broader cultural practice in which children are reified and objectified. This is not meant to suggest that all child beauty pageants constitute a form of child abuse. Pageants vary both in the way they are constructed and in how they interact with local and national audiences. Moreover, their outcomes are variable and contingent. But beauty pageants, as sites of representation, identity formation, consumption, and regulation, have to be understood in terms of how they articulate and resonate with other cultural sites engaged in the production and regulation of youth, the packaging of desire, and the sexualized body.

BEAUTY PAGEANTS AND THE SHOCK OF THE REAL

The Ramsey case challenges and disrupts ideological conventions that typically apply to narratives of childhood innocence. The blitz of media coverage following the brutal murder of six-year-old JonBenet Ramsey gives evidence to that fact. On one level, Jon-Benet's case attracted national attention because it fed into the frenzy and moral panic Americans are experiencing over the threat of child abuse—fueled by horrific crimes like the kidnap and murder of Polly Klaas in California. Similarly, it resonated with the highly charged public campaigns of various legislators and citizen groups calling for the death penalty for sex offenders such as Jesse Timmendequas, the child molester who killed seven-year-old Megan Kanka. On another level, it opened to public scrutiny another high-profile example of a child succeeding at the make-believe game of becoming an adult. Not unlike Jessica Dubroff, the seven-year-old would-be Amelia Earhart who, while attempting to be the youngest pilot to cross the United States, died in a plane crash, JonBenet Ramsey also projected the uncanny ability to present herself as an adult. But if the boundary between innocence and impurity, child and adult, became blurred in both cases, JonBenet's notoriety as an object of public fascination revealed a dark and seamy element in American culture.

Night after night the major television networks aired videotapes of little JonBenet Ramsey in a tight, off-the-shoulder dress, bright red lipstick, and teased, bleached blond hair pulling a feathered Mardi Gras mask coyly across her eyes as she sashayed down a runway. Playing the role of an alluring sex kitten, JonBenet seemed to belie the assumption that the voyeuristic fascination with the sexualized child was confined to the margins of society, inhabited largely by freaks and psychopaths.

The JonBenet Ramsey case revealed not only how regressive notions of femininity and beauty are redeployed in this conservative era to fashion the fragile identities of young girls but also how easily adults will project their own fantasies onto children, even if it means selling them on the beauty block. The JonBenet case offered the public a spectacle in which it became both a voyeur and a witness to its own refusal to address the broader conditions that contribute to the sexualization and commercialization of kids in the culture at large. The general public has come to recognize that child abuse often takes place at home and that the conventional image of the molester as an outsider is less than credible thanks to the recent attention given to child abuse by celebrities such as Roseanne Barr and Oprah Winfrey. The view of the home as a safe space for children also became questionable, as it became clear that the Ramseys imposed their own strange fantasies on their daughter and in doing so denied her an identity suitable for a six-year-old. Instead, they positioned her within a child beauty pageant culture that stripped her of her innocence by blurring the boundary between child and adult. Not allowed to be a child, JonBenet was given the unfortunate job of projecting herself through a degrading aesthetic that sexualized and commodified her. Collapsing the (hardly clear-cut) boundaries between the protective parental gaze and the more objectified adult gaze, JonBenet's parents appear to have stripped their daughter of any sense of agency, independence, or autonomy in order to remake her in the image of their own desires and pleasures. Parental "care" in this case appears to have been wielded tyrannically to prevent JonBenet from experiencing childhood pleasures and needs outside the gaze of pleasure-seeking, narcissistic adults.

Images of six-year-olds cosmetically transformed into sultry, Lolita-like waifs are difficult to watch. They strike at the heart of a culture deeply disturbed in its alleged respect for children and decency. Whereas the blame for the often-violent consequences associated with this eroticized costuming is usually placed on young women, it is hard to blame JonBenet Ramsey for this type of objectification. The public's usual attacks on kids suggesting that they are responsible for society's ills breaks down in this case as it becomes more difficult for adults to evade responsibility for what they do to children—their own and others.[14] JonBenet's image violently transgresses a sacred responsibility associated with protecting the innocence of children. Writ large across the media coverage of the JonBenet case was the disturbing implication and recognition that childhood innocence is tarnished when children can no longer expect "protection . . . consistency and some sort of dignity" from adults.[15]

The JonBenet Ramsey case prompted an unusual debate in the media and national press. Lacking the theoretical tools or political will to analyze the institutional and ideological forces in the culture that generate such disregard for children, the media focused on what was often termed "the strange subculture of child beauty pageants." More often than not it suggested that the abuse children suffered in such pageants was due to overbearing mothers trying to control their daughters' lives. It seems that if young girls are unavailable for scapegoating, their mothers will suffice. Rarely did the media raise the larger issue of how young girls are being educated to function within such a limited sphere of cultural life or how such a regressive education for young girls is more often the norm rather than the exception.

The traditional moral guardians of children's culture who would censor rap lyrics, remove "dangerous" videos and CDs from public circulation, boycott Disney for pro-gay and lesbian labor practices, and empty school libraries of many classic texts have had little to say about the sexualization of young children in children's beauty pageants, a social form as American as apple pie. Nor are they willing to acknowledge that such pageants must be considered within a broader set of practices which increasingly includes youth sport events that appeal to middle- and upper-class parents who seem willing to sacrifice their children's welfare to the imperatives of success and celebrity. Amid the silence of conservatives and the family values crowd, liberal and progressive reporters have begun to raise some important questions. For example, CBS anchorman Dan Rather criticized the television networks for running the JonBenet tapes, claiming that they amounted to nothing less than kiddy porn.

Columnist Frank Rich wrote a courageous piece in the *New York Times* in which he argued that the "strange world of kids' pageantry is not a 'subculture'—it's our culture. But as long as we call it a subculture, it can remain a problem for somebody else."[16] Reporter Richard Goldstein followed up Rich's insights with a three-part series in *The Village Voice* in which he argued that the marketing of the sexual child has a long history in the United States and that the JonBenet case "brings to the surface both our horror at how effectively a child can be constructed as a sexual being and our guilt at the pleasure we take in such a sight."[17] For Goldstein, the JonBenet case challenges the American public to confront the actual nature of child abuse, which is all too often a part of family life and is further legitimated by a culture willing to capitalize on children as the new arena for the production of pleasure and commercial exploitation.

All of these critiques raise valid concerns about the role of child beauty pageants and how they produce particular notions of beauty, pleasure, and femininity that are as culturally gender-specific as they are degrading. Such criticisms also prompt a debate about the nature of adult needs and desires that push kids into pageants, and how such pageants correspond with other social practices that "silently" reproduce roles for children that undermine the notion of child innocence and reinforce particular forms of child abuse. In what follows, I examine these issues in detail by focusing on the scope and popularity of children's beauty pageants, what they attempt to teach young girls, and the broader commercial forces that sustain them. I also locate the phenomenon of child beauty pageants within a broader, related set of cultural practices, especially the world of high-fashion advertising and the rise of the teenage model.

BEAUTY AND THE BEAST:
A GENEALOGY OF CHILD BEAUTY PAGEANTS

Frank Rich is on target in arguing that child beauty pageants represent more than a subculture in American society. Ted Cohen, president of World Pageants Inc., which publishes an international directory of pageants, estimates that the pageantry industry represents a billion-dollar-a-year industry, with sponsors such as Procter and Gamble, Black Velvet, and Hawaiian Tropics.[18] An estimated 3,000 pageants a year are held in the United States in which more than 100,000 children under the age of twelve compete.[19] In some cases, girls as young as eight months are entered in pageants. California, Florida, and New York hold the most pageants, and the number of pageants in the United States appears to be growing, despite the fact that many contests, especially at the national level, charge entrants between $250 and $800.[20] Most contestants who enter local pageants are from working-class families driven by mobility fantasies and the lure of a small cash prize. The larger and more expensive pageants appear to be dominated by middle- and upper-class parents like the Ramseys, who have lots of money and resources to spend on costly voice and dance lessons, pageant coaches, expensive costumes, and entry fees.[21]

Pageants are a lucrative business. Promoters market prurient pleasure and rake in big dividends, with some making as much as $100,000 on each event. In addition, child beauty pageants have produced a number of support industries, including costume designers, grooming consultants, interview coaches, photographers, and publishers,[22] not to mention the cosmetics, weight reduction, and other "beauty-aid industries." Trade magazines such as Pageant Life, which has a circulation of 60,000, offer their readers images and advertisements celebrating ideals of femininity, glamour, and beauty while marketing young girls in the image of adult drives and desires. In some cases, parents invest big money for makeup artists, hairstylists, and coaches to teach prepubescent kids particular "pro-am modeling styles and tornado spins."[23] A story that appeared in Life magazine in 1994 featuring Blaire, an eleven-year-old seasoned beauty pageant performer, documented this trend. Blaire's fortunes at winning got better when her mom and dad hired Tony, a voice coach and makeup artist, who charges $40 an hour, to completely redesign her. When Blaire's father was asked why he was so involved with entering Blaire in child beauty pageants, he answered: "I am a plastic surgeon only from the neck up. I enjoy the beauty of the face. No doubt that's why I am so involved with Blaire." The article reports that "Bruce is captivated by his daughter's beauty but prefers it enhanced: He apologizes to strangers when she is not wearing makeup. Some parents have accused Bruce of enhancing Blaire's looks with surgery." Blaire indicates that she loves pageants; they are all she is interested in. The article ends by pointing out that Blaire lacks a child's spontaneity and then conjectures that she "shows so little offstage emotion because she's so busy editing herself with adults."[24]

Blaire's case may appear to some a caricature of pageant life, narrowly depicting parents who push their kids too hard and who impose their own interests and desires on children too young to decide whether they actually want to participate in the pageants. But the popular literature is replete with such stories. Many parents involved in these pageants do not seem concerned about the possible negative consequences of dressing their children in provocative clothing, capping their teeth, putting fake eyelashes on them, and having them perform before audiences in a manner that suggests a sexuality well beyond their years.

The popular literature that supports the child beauty pageant culture fails to acknowledge that "sexualized images of little girls may have dangerous implications in a world where 450,000 American children were reported as victims of sexual abuse in 1993."[25] Trade magazines such as *Pageant Life* and *Babette's Pageant and Talent Gazette* are filled with ads in which toddlers strike suggestive poses. Full-page spreads of contest finalists depict contestants ranging in age from two to twenty-four years. All of the entrants are defined by the same aesthetic: the makeup, pose, smile, and hairstyles of the six-year-olds are no different from those of the young women. Within the beauty pageant aesthetic, the line between children and adults is blurred; all of the images depict the cool estrangement of sexual allure that has become a trademark of the commodities industry. In addition, the magazines are full of ads hawking outfits from companies called, for example, "Hollywood Babe" and "Little Starlet Fashions"—with many ads invoking the warning "Don't Be Left Behind."[26] One even gushes that contestants may enter a particular pageant for the fee of only $1.00 per pound. Success stories for the younger-age set (four- to eight-year-olds) consistently focus on the thrill of competition, on winning titles, and on the successful modeling careers of the pageant winners.

Parents and pageant sponsors often respond to public criticisms by arguing that the press overreacted to JonBenet Ramsey's death by unfairly focusing on beauty pageants as somehow being implicated in her murder. Others legitimate the child beauty pageant culture as a route to get their kids into lucrative careers such as modeling or to win college scholarships, financial awards, and other prizes. The most frequently used rationale for defending pageants is that they build self-esteem in children, "help them to overcome shyness, and [teach them how] to grow up."[27] One pageant director in Murrieta, California, refuted the criticism that pageants are detrimental for young girls, arguing that "many young girls look at pageants as a protracted game of dress up, something most young girls love."[28] Pam Griffin, another pageant proponent, whose daughter trained JonBenet Ramsey, remarked that "more girls are trying pageants after seeing how much fun JonBenet had."[29] Even *Vogue* reporter Ellen Mark concluded that most kids who participate in beauty pageants end up as success stories. The reason for their success, according to Mark, is that "pageants made them feel special. . . . Little girls like to look pretty."[30]

This argument, in appropriating the ideology of liberal feminism, emphasizes that girls gain affirming self-direction, autonomy, and a strong competitive spirit through their participation in pageants. But such critiques often fail to recognize that self-esteem is actually being defined within a very narrow standard of autonomy, one that is impervious to how gender is continually made and remade within a politics of appearance that is often reduced to the level of a degrading spectacle. Self-esteem in this context means embracing rather than critically challenging a gender code that rewards little girls for their looks, submissiveness, and sex appeal. Coupled with the ways in which the broader culture, through television, music, magazines, and advertising, consistently bombards young girls with a sexualized ideal of femininity "from which all threatening elements have been purged,"[31] self-esteem often becomes a euphemism for self-hatred, rigid gender roles, and powerlessness.

There is a certain irony in appropriating the language of self-esteem to defend child beauty pageants, especially since the pageants provide young children with standards of beauty that 1 of 40,000 young women will actually meet. Must we ask what is wrong with young girls wanting to become fashion models who increasingly look as if they will never grow up (e.g., Kate Moss), and for whom beauty is not only defined by the male gaze but appears to be one of the few requisites to enter "into the privileged male world."[32] Feminist theorist Naomi Wolf is right in arguing that the problem with linking standardized notions of sexualized beauty to self-esteem is that it does not present young girls or adult women with many choices. This is especially true when issues regarding sexual pleasure and self-determination are held hostage to notions of femininity in which it becomes difficult for women to move beyond such infantilized representations in order to express themselves in ways that are empowering.[33] Moreover, on the other side of the cheap glamorization of the waif-child as the fashion icon of beauty is the reality of a patriarchal society in which the nymphet fantasy reveals a "system by which men impose their authority on women and children alike."[34]

In short, rarely do the defenders of child beauty pageants address the consequences of stealing away a child's innocence by portraying her as a sexualized nymphet. Once again, they have little to say about what children are actually learning in pageants, how a child might see herself and mediate her relationship to society when her sense of self-worth is defined largely through a notion of beauty that is one-dimensional and demeaning. Nor do parents and other pageant participators seem to question the wisdom of allowing children to be sponsored by corporations. The message that often informs such relations is that the identities of the young girls who enter the pageants become meaningful only when tied to the logic of the market. What a young girl learns is that "in order to enter [the] contest she must represent someone other than herself."[35]

Unlike contests that took place ten or fifteen years ago, pageants, especially the national ones, now offer bigger prizes and are backed by corporate sponsors. Moreover, as the commercial interests and level of investment have risen, so have their competitive nature, hype, and glitz. V. J. LaCour, publisher of *Pageant Life Magazine* and a firm supporter of child beauty pageants, thinks that many parents have resorted to makeup and other "extreme" measures because "the parents are trying to get a competitive edge."[36] In some cases, parents resort to mentally punitive and physically cruel practices to get their kids to perform "properly." Lois Miller, owner of the Star Talent Management in Allentown, Pennsylvania, reports that she has "seen parents who have pinched their children for messing up their dress or not looking appropriate or not wiggling enough or not throwing kisses."[37] Parents often respond to such criticisms by claiming that their kids are doing exactly what they want to do and that they enjoy being in the pageants. This argument is strained when parents enter children as young as eight months into pageants, or when parents decide, as reported in *Money* magazine, that their four-year-old child needed a talent agent to make the "right connections" outside of the beauty pageants.

Sixty Minutes, the television program highly acclaimed for its investigative reporting, aired a segment on child beauty pageants on May 18, 1997, in the aftermath of the JonBenet Ramsey controversy. The premise of the program, announced by commentator Morley Safer, was to explore whether "child beauty pageants exploit children to satisfy ambitions of parents." To provide a historical perspective on such pageants, *Sixty Minutes* aired cuts from child beauty pageants that had been seen on the program in 1977 and then presented videotaped shots of JonBenet and other children performing in a recent pageant. The contrast was both obscene and informative. The children in the 1977 pageants wore little-girl dresses and ribbons in their hair; they embodied a childlike innocence as they displayed their little-girl talents— singing, tap, and baton twirling. Not so with the more recent pageant shots. The contestants did not look like little girls but rather like coquettish young women whose talents were reduced to an ability to move suggestively across the stage. Clearly, as Morley Safer indicated, "By today's beauty pageant standards, innocence seems to have vanished." When he asked one of the stage mothers who had appeared in the 1977 program what she thought of today's pageants, she responded that she recently went to a child beauty pageant and "walked in the door and walked out. It was disgusting to see the beaded dresses and blown-up hair on kids." The program's take on child beauty pageants was critical, yet it failed to consider the broader social practices, representations, and relations of power that provide the context for such pageants to flourish in the United States. Nor did it analyze the growing popularity of the pageants as part of a growing backlash against feminism reproduced in the media, culture, and fashion industries as well as in a growing number of conservative economic and political establishments.[38] Morley Safer was, however, clear about the assumption that the root of such abuse toward children was to be placed squarely on the shoulders of overly ambitious and exploitative mothers.

The feminist backlash has not stopped more informed criticisms from emerging. For example, some child psychologists argue that the intense competition at pageants compounded with the nomadic lifestyle of traveling from one hotel to another when school is not in session make it difficult for young children to make friends, putting them at risk for developing problems in social interactions with other children. Other child specialists argue that it is as developmentally inappropriate to "teach a six-year-old to pose like a twenty-year-old model as it is to allow her to drive [and] drink alcohol."[39] Of course, there is also the stress of competition and the danger of undermining a child's self-confidence, especially when she loses, if the message she receives is that how she looks is the most important aspect of who she is. Psychologist David Elkind argues that parents used to be concerned with the ethical behavior of kids. A decade ago, when kids got home from school, their parents asked them if they were good. Now, because of the new economic realities of downsizing and deindustrialization, parents are fearful that their kids will be losers.[40] Parents, too often, now focus on how well their kids are competing. Journalist Marly Harris writes that the "massive restructuring of the economy creates a winner-take-all society in which parents believe that if kids don't end up as one of the few winners they will join the ranks of the many losers."[41] Thus the question kids get when they come home in the 1990s is no longer "Have you been good?" but "Did you win?" The message here is did you get the highest grades? Harris also believes that the money spent on child pageants by parents, up to $10,000 per child a year in some cases, could be invested in more productive ways, say in savings plans to help them finance the cost of a college education. But the attributes that are accentuated when defining their identities and self-esteem offer them limited opportunities to develop and express themselves.[42]

In spite of such criticisms, child beauty pageants are enormously popular in the United States, and their popularity is growing. Moreover, they have their defenders.[43] In part, such popularity can be explained, as I mentioned previously, by their potential to make money for promoters, but there is more to the story. Children's beauty contests also represent places where the rituals of small-town America combine with the ideology of mass consumer culture. Pageants with titles such as "Miss Catfish Queen," "Miss Baby Poultry Princess," and "The Snake Charmer

Queen Ritual Competition" suggest that such rituals are easily adapted to "local meanings and familiar symbols, values, and aesthetics—those relevant to the producers, performers, and consumers of the contest."[44] Such rituals are easy to put on; are advertised as a legitimate form of family entertainment; resonate powerfully with dominant Western models of femininity, beauty, and culture; and play a crucial role at local and national levels of reproducing particular notions of citizenship and national identity. Child beauty pageants are often embraced as simply good, clean entertainment and defended for their civic value to the community. Moreover, while adult beauty contests, such as the annual Miss America pageant, have been the target of enormous amounts of feminist criticism,[45] few academics and cultural critics have focused on child beauty pageants as a serious object of cultural analysis.[46]

BEYOND THE POLITICS OF CHILD ABUSE

Any attempt to challenge the sexist practices and abuses at work in children's beauty pageants must begin with the recognition that pageants represent more than trivial entertainment. Educational theorist Valerie Walkerdine argued that forms of popular culture such as the beauty pageant offer a way for working-class girls to escape the limiting discourses and ideologies found in schools and other institutions. Popular culture becomes a realm of fantasy offering the promise of escape, possibility, and personal triumph. Desire in this instance gains expression through an endless parade of highly sexualized images and narratives that not only provide the promise of erotic fantasies that "belong to them" but also constitute for these young girls an important strategy for survival.[47] According to Walkerdine, popular cultural forms such as child beauty pageants occupy a reputable public space in which preadolescent working-class girls are offered forms of identification they can appropriate as survival practices in a society stacked against them. But what Walkerdine ignores is that such fantasies often are founded on forms of identification and hope that offer nothing more than the swindle of fulfillment, providing limited choices and options to young girls. Moreover, while such strategies cannot be dismissed as politically incorrect but must be considered within a broader understanding of how desire is both mediated and acted upon, the social costs for such identifications go far beyond the benefits they provide as a buffer against hard times. In the long run, such investments serve to limit, often exploit, and disrupt working-class lives. At the same time, the emergence of cultural forms such as the child beauty pageant makes clear the degree to which viable public spheres are diminishing for children. As public funding decreases, support services dry up, and extracurricular activities are eliminated from schools because of financial shortages, society contains very few noncommercial public spaces for young people to identify with and experience. As market relations expand their control over public space, corporations increasingly provide the public spheres for children to experience themselves as consuming subjects and commodities with limited opportunities to learn how to develop their full range of intellectual and emotional capacities to be critical citizens.

While many progressives are well aware that the struggle over culture is tantamount to the struggle over meaning and identity, it is also important to recognize that any viable cultural politics also must locate specific cultural texts within wider relations of power that shape everyday life. Understood within a broader set of relations, child beauty pageants become an important object of critical analysis for a number of reasons. First, the conservative and rigid gender roles that are legitimated at many child beauty pageants must be analyzed both in terms of the specific ideologies they construct for children and how these ideologies find expression in other parts of the culture. What I want to suggest is that the values and dominant motifs that shape beauty pageants gain their meaning and appeal precisely because they find expression in related cultural spheres throughout American society. For instance, by examining advertising campaigns such as those produced by Calvin Klein or in the increasing use of advertising that depicts the ideal modern American female as young, extremely thin, sexually alluring, and available, it becomes clear that the processes at work in the objectification of young children are not altogether different from the social relations that take place in other sites. All of these sites use the bodies and body parts of young girls to market desire and sell goods. What often makes such connections untenable in the public eye is that beauty pageants appropriate innocence as a trope for doing what is best for children, often in the name of dominant family values. And yet, it is precisely in the name of innocence that practices that might be seen in other contexts as abusive to children are defined within the dominant culture as simply good, clean, family entertainment.

In advertisements for Calvin Klein's Obsession perfume and in his more recent jeans ads, innocence becomes a fractured sign and is used unapologetically to present children as the objects of desire and adults as voyeurs. Innocence in this instance feeds into enticing images of childlike purity as it simultaneously sexualizes and markets such images. Sexualizing children may be the final frontier in the fashion world, exemplified by the rise of models such as Kate Moss who represent the ideal woman as a waif—-sticklike, expressionless, and blank-eyed.[48] Or it simply makes celebrities out of teenage models such as Ivanka Trump, who in their waning teen years are left wondering if they are too old to have a career in those culture industries that reduce a woman's talents to elusive and short-lived standards of desire, sexuality, and beauty. What connects the beauty pageants to the world of advertising and fashion modeling is that young girls are being taught to become little women, while women are being taught to assume the identities of powerless, childlike waifs. In this instance, Lolita grows up only to retreat into her youth as a model for what it means to be a woman.[49] Here innocence reveals a dark quality; not only are youth being assaulted across a variety of public spaces but their identities, especially those of young women, are being appropriated in different ways in diverse public sites for the high pleasure quotient they evoke in satisfying adult desires and needs.

As an ethical referent, innocence humanizes children and makes a claim on adults to provide them with security and protection. But innocence gains its meaning from a complex set of semiotic, material, and social registers. And what is happening to children in many cultural spheres as seemingly unrelated as child beauty pageants and the world of advertising and fashion modeling suggests how vulnerable children actually are to learning the worst social dimensions of our society: misogyny, sexism, racism, and violence. Innocence needs to be understood as a metaphor that is open to diverse uses and whose effects can be both positive and devastating for children. If innocence is to become a useful category for social analysis, the term must be understood politically and ethically only through the ways in which it is represented and used within everyday life, shaped by language, representations, and the technologies of power. Central to analyzing a politics of innocence the need to address why, how, and under what conditions the marketing of children's bodies increasingly permeates diverse elements of society. Likewise, educators and others must uncover not only the political and ideological interests and relations of power at work in the construction of innocence but also the actual ways in which cultural practices are deployed to influence how children and adults learn about themselves and their relationships to others.

Innocence becomes both a mystifying ideology and a vehicle for commercial profit. In the first instance, innocence is a highly charged term that points to pedophiles and sexual perverts as the most visible threats to children in our society. Such a restricted notion of innocence fails to understand how child abuse connects to and works its way through the most seemingly benign of cultural spheres such as the beauty pageant. Thus beauty pageants are not only ignored as serious objects of social analysis but are dismissed as simply a subculture. Here innocence protects a particular notion of family values that is class specific and racially coded. In a society in which working-class youth and youth of color are represented as a threat and menace to public order, innocence becomes an ideological trope defined through its contrast with children who are constructed as "other." Innocence as ideological trope reinforces a politics of innocence that legitimates the cultural capital of children who are largely white, middle class, and privileged. Moreover, the discourse of innocence provides little understanding of how the conditions under which children learn in specific places resonate and gain legitimacy through their connection to other cultural sites.

In the second instance, innocence falls prey to the logic of the market and the successful teaching operations of consumerism. The myth of innocence is increasingly appropriated through a glitzy aesthetic in which children provide the sexualized bait that creates images and representations that tread close to the border of pornography. In this scenario, children's sense of play and their social development are transformed through marketing strategies and forms of consumer education that define the limits of their imaginations, identities, and sense of possibility while simultaneously providing through the electronic media a "kind of entertainment that subtly influence[s] the way we see [children], ourselves, and our communities."[50]

Concerned educators, parents, and activists must begin to challenge and counter such images, ideologies, and social practices as part of a cultural politics that makes issues of teaching and power central to its project. This means taking seriously how beauty pageants and other popular cultural sites teach children to think of themselves through the representations, values, and languages offered to them.[51] It also means expanding our understanding of how education is played out on the bodies of young children in pageants and how this practice resonates with what children are taught in other cultural spheres. Schools and other educational sites must treat popular culture as a serious area of analysis. This suggests teaching kids and adults how to read popular culture critically. It also means teaching them how to be cultural producers capable of using new technologies to create texts that honor and critically engage their traditions and experiences. In strategic terms, students must be offered texts, resources, and strategies that provide a complex range of subject positions that they can address, inhabit, mediate, and experiment with. Students and adults also should be taught how to organize social movements at the local and national levels to pressure and boycott companies that engage in abusive practices toward children. Underlying this merging of the political and the educational is the overt political goal of "enabling people to act more strategically in ways that may change their context for the better"[52] and the educational goal of finding ways for diverse groups of children and adults to work together to transform popular public spheres into sites that address social problems by way of democratic, rather than merely market, considerations.[53]

In short, the socialization of children must be addressed within a larger discussion about citizenship and democracy, one that resists what philosopher Theodor Adorno calls the "obscene merger of aesthetics and reality."[54] What Adorno means here is precisely the refutation of those ideologies and social practices that attempt to subordinate, if not eliminate, forms of identity fundamental to public life, to an economy of bodies and pleasures that is all surface and spectacle. Such a discussion not only calls into question the conditions under which kids learn, what they learn, and how this knowledge shapes their identities and behavior, it also raises questions about the material and institutional relations of power that are fundamental for maintaining the integrity of public life—a condition that is essential for all children to learn in order to be critical participants in the shaping of their lives and the larger social order. Child abuse comes in many forms, and it has become a disturbing feature of American society. The current assault being waged on children through retrograde policy, the dismantling of the welfare state, and the pervasive glut of images that cast them as the principal incitements to adult desire suggest that democracy is in the throes of a major crisis. If democracy is to carry us forward into the next century, surely it will be based on a commitment to improving the lives of children, but not within the degrading logic of a market that treats their bodies as commodities and their futures as trade-offs for capital accumulation. On the contrary, critical educators and other progressives need to create a cultural vision and a set of strategies informed by "the rhetoric of political, civic, and economic citizenship."[55] The challenge to take up that commitment has never been so strained nor so urgent.

TWO

Heroin Chic
and the Politics of Seduction

INTRODUCTION

It is the fear of what Jean Baudrillard calls simulations
without referents, a Disneyland society in which unan-
chored desires float from object to object at the dictate
of consumer capitalism. The body in such a society loses
its material reality; pain ceases to be a teacher, and
pleasure is degraded to mere stimulation.
                                    —Richard Sennett, "The Social Body"

In the postmodern world described by philosopher Jean Baudrillard
daily life consists of an endless series of simulations that lack any
concrete referents. Disneyland becomes a model for a sanitized
society purged of politics, a society in which representations
become increasingly homogenized and cease to be read critically as
part of a broader strategy of understanding, struggle, and intervention.[1] In this mediascape, images bombard the senses, identities
become transparent and one-dimensional, space and time collapse
and displace traditional understandings of place and history, and

concrete reality slips into a virtual society where "there is more and more information, and less and less meaning."[2]

Postmodern culture has become less a mode of cultural criticism than a political and social condition marked by the rise of the national entertainment state and the spread of corporate culture into every facet of life.[3] The concentration of apparatuses of cultural production, organization, and distribution in fewer and fewer hands undermines the possibility for culture to be a dynamic zone of contention, an active public space prompting dialogue, dissent, and critical engagement. Culture becomes instead a commercial public sphere marked by the emergence, if not the triumph, of stylized and superficial forms. Within such a society, "the social turns itself into advertising . . . and all current forms of activity tend toward advertising and most exhaust themselves therein."[4] As the social is emptied of all political and ethical referents, the tension between entertainment and politics becomes blurred, just as the relationship between art and commerce becomes less controversial.

It would be comforting to believe that Baudrillard's world of simulations exists simply as an arcane theoretical discourse endlessly replayed at academic conferences or Las Vegas retreats.[5] But the logic of simulation—with its indifference to the distinction between representations of reality and actual experiences—operates in a variety of public spaces. In those spaces the social imaginary is redefined and reproduced within a commercial logic that renounces all claims to politics, moral compassion, and the obligations of public life. In such a society art and commerce increasingly combine to package identities, commodify bodies as objects of commerce, and organize desires according to the dictates of the market. Creativity is given free reign as long as it sells goods; it no longer serves to connect artistic transgression with political resistance or democratic struggles.

As culture is increasingly shaped by the market, artists and other cultural workers can comfortably mortgage themselves to the logic of late capitalism and engage the larger society not as agents of social responsibility but as public relations intellectuals. For instance, film directors such as Francis Ford Coppola and Ridley Scott surrender their critical sensibilities and auteur status in order to work for corporate giants such as Disney, producing films that dissolve politics into either white-bread comedy or high-octane, military machismo (i.e., *Jack* and *G.I. Jane*). Numerous contemporary artists have followed in Andy Warhol's footsteps, using their talents to produce ads for, among other items, Absolut Vodka.[6] Similarly, the clothing company Benetton displays its ads in various galleries and employs a variety of actors and artists to either endorse or work for the company. Besides blurring the line between culture and society, such artists and companies purge artistic production of any ethical referent while reaffirming the victory of capital over human compassion: Social responsibility loses out to the imperatives of the bottom line.

In a postmodern world, consumption rather than production drives the capitalist economy. Within this new capitalist formation, culture is more than commercialized, it is emptied of resistance as critical reflection gives way to the reified image of the spectacle. Failing to discern the difference between reality as a fact and reality as a possibility, between a morality committed to addressing forms of oppression and a representative politics in which oppression, suffering, and despair are translated into a stylized aesthetic, the market-driven cultural realm demonstrates an apocalyptic emptiness. As the machineries of cultural pedagogy extend beyond the school into the largely corporate-controlled, electronically based media of communication, the realities of personal experience and collective memory are transformed into a "cartoon utopia" dressed up as entertainment.[7]

Within such a representational politics, commerce emerges as the bearer of a "refreshing" kind of art—a new form of cultural production elevating the aesthetic as its most important organizing principle. Culture and commodity become indistinguishable, and social identities are shaped almost exclusively within the ideology of consumerism. This is particularly clear in the way in which popular fashion designers have used talented photographers such as Steven Meisel and Richard Avedon to recast or reframe indignation and resistance as no more than an attachment to a perfume, pair of jeans, shirt, or "something as distant, and as decorative, as an alligator."[8]

The representational politics and relations of power that connect art and commerce veil how the operations of power work to produce public spaces in which identities are shaped, values are learned, and social relations are legitimated. Of course, many artists, cultural critics, and social theorists have begun to explore this issue in the second half of the twentieth century. What is new is not the intersection of art and commerce but the degree to which, as exemplified by "heroin chic," politics dissolves into pathology. I refer here to an exclusively aesthetic sensibility in which the experience of drug addiction and poverty become simply representations linking the emotionally charged stimulus of the spectacle to the free-floating desires of consumer capitalism. Within such a representational politics, aesthetics replaces any vestige of a moral sensibility while simultaneously restricting the public space and sense of agency offered to young people and others. But the aesthetic of heroin chic legitimates not only a cynical disdain for human suffering, it also functions as a retro-aesthetic in which subcultural politics—however nihilistic and pathological—provide the new disposable marketing pose for making profits. Transgression in this instance either reproduces uncritically or sanctions what art critic Carol Becker has called "manifestations of psychic unhealth—malaise, racism, hypocrisy, despair."[9]

In what follows, I argue that the emergence in the mid-1990s of the heroin chic controversy in the popular press offers an important example of how art and commerce meet to rewrite the politics of transgression or resistance as a domesticated mode of address designed to produce a consuming rather than a critical, social subject. Not only does the heroin chic controversy reveal how transgression is purged of any semblance of political resistance, it demonstrates how such "transgression" becomes domesticated and complicitous by positioning its audience as voyeurs who can pleasurably consume prevailing sexist, racist, and class specific stereotypes about youth and women. Social critic Richard Sennett signals the domestication of resistance by arguing that "the politics of transgression envisions a resistance to the norms of the dominant society which does nothing to change the social rules themselves. And even at best, the discourse of transgression evokes a familiar cultural trope: freedom as the mentality of alienation."[10]

I also want to argue that the "new art" of heroin chic in fashion photography points to a politics of representation that must be understood in relation to the current right-wing assault on working-class youth and women. Heroin chic does more than maximize the pleasure of viewing by glamorizing the aesthetics of cultural slumming; it also reinforces a cynicism that permeates large parts of the public sector in which the bodies of youth and women are no longer viewed within the privileged space of possibility. Agency in this view is devoid of any sense of possibility. Bodies presented within stylized images that are anorexic, physically abused, and paralyzed from substance abuse do not evoke sympathy or compassion but work largely to reinforce our image of youth as symbols of violence, crime, and social disorder and women as simply sexualized commodities.

Finally, I want to propose that the emergence of a society marked by an ever-increasing commodification and homogeneity of culture does not and should not suggest that political resistance is meaningless. On the contrary, the sites of political struggle as well as the strategies employed by progressive cultural workers must be rethought and seized upon within new forms of struggle and resistance. Domination is never total in its effects; contradictions arise within all public spaces, even those that appear to be the most oppressive. While such a recognition in and of itself does not change anything, it is a precondition for educational and political work that deepens our understanding of the role artists who work primarily in the cultural sphere, i.e., cultural workers might play alone and collectively in revitalizing democratic public life.

HEROIN AND THE POLITICS OF POPULAR CULTURE

I saw the best minds of my generation destroyed by madness, starving hysterical naked, dragging themselves through the negro streets at dawn looking for an angry fix.

—*Alan Ginsburg, "Howl," 1956*

The highs and lows of heroin use and addiction have a long legacy in popular culture and mass media. A lineage extending from writer William Burroughs and musician Lou Reed to the musical groups the Sex Pistols and Jane's Addiction gave heroin use a cult status that extends from the 1950s to the present. This is exemplified in the work of photographer and film director Larry Clark, and extends from his seminal 1970 photo-essay *Tulsa* to his more recent films, *Kids* and *Another Day in Paradise.* Heroin's bohemian image was amplified as well as tempered by the deaths of such rock stars as Janis Joplin and Jerry Garcia and of Hollywood actors John Belushi and River Phoenix. Grunge rockers found both an idol and a tragic example of heroin use in the legacy and suicide of Kurt Cobain. But rock also produced an endless array of heroin survivors, such as some of the members of Aerosmith, who provided gruesome confessionals about addiction and abuse. Ironically, such confessionals seemed to increase heroin's rising appeal to middle-class kids by suggesting that one could use the drug over long periods of time and still survive, thus undermining the equation of junk and death. The longevity of Patti Smith, Marianne Faithfull,

Iggy Pop, and Keith Richards make them icons of junk culture, revered because of their personal journey through the ultimate antiestablishment ritual.

Hollywood has offered its celluloid version of heroin's rhythms in recent films such as *Drugstore Cowboy, Pulp Fiction, Trainspotting,* and *Another Day in Paradise. Trainspotting,* one of the most controversial films to deal with heroin in the 1990s, spearheaded its advertising campaign with the memorable line: "Take the best orgasm you ever had. Multiply it by a thousand. You're still nowhere near it." But drug films such as *Trainspotting* and *Gridlock'd* also showed the downside of heroin addiction. In the art world, Nan Goldin produced numerous photographs chronicling the ups and downs of her friends' habits, addictions, and deaths in the 1970s and 1980s. The representational politics of junk culture before the 1990s not only posited itself at the outpost of bohemian culture, it also paid lip service to creating or inhabiting new spaces where identity, place, and pleasure could be released from the demands of the dominant society.

No single narrative does justice to the complexity of heroin use among a generation of returning Vietnam War veterans, bohemians, and cultural outlaws that populated the cultural landscape of marginalized urban haunts before the rise of heroin chic in the 1990s. Yet I do think it is possible to suggest that the legacy of the 1960s offered rationales for heroin use. Experience did not disassociate itself from meaning as much as it rushed headlong into a search for transcendence in which meaning and affect were redefined as part of a journey beyond middle-class norms and values. When not prompted by poverty, human suffering, and the heroin epidemic spawned by the Vietnam War,[11] heroin use found its rationale among intellectuals, artists, and other marginal groups not within the confines of fashion but as a dead-end politics that weighed existential freedom against a potentially self-destructive act. The romance of heroin use was never that far removed from the recognition of the "damage done" and the lives it destroyed.

In the 1990s, heroin became the drug of choice for upper-middle-class professionals who did not want to compromise their power or advantaged social positions but who wanted to escape from the boredom of their lives by entering into a junk culture that romanticized the dangers and risks associated with the street culture of the dispossessed and poor. Appearing as the ultimate form of transgression, heroin use in the mid-1990s became a cultural signifier among the rich, famous, and trendy for combining the cool posture of alienation and the chilling willingness to appropriate what was considered *the* outlaw fashion accessory.[12] What is often left out of this narrative is that heroin also has become increasingly popular among middle-class kids, especially high schoolers and older teens.[13]

Current heroin use has to be understood not just as the dangerous posturing of the bored and curious but also as a pernicious symbol of despair and pessimism that the mass media uses to falsely characterize an entire generation of young people for whom adult society appears to be not only morally indifferent but also vindictive. Seen as both troubled and troubling, youth appear as a burden, if not a threat, to public life. This view ignores the realities of a generation of youth plagued by deindustrialization, downsizing, unemployment, and the dismantling of the welfare state. Such factors have created fundamentally new realities for young people: a future of dead-end jobs, few social benefits, and the menacing image of a state mobilizing ever-expanding apparatuses of surveillance and containment. Young people recognize the growing threat of the state so clearly that high-gloss magazines, such as *Details*, attempting to cater to the ideas and perceptions of youth, run Diesel jeans ads that turn an ugly state of affairs into the object of satire. A recent Diesel ad portrays a number of young people dressed in jeans, hosing themselves down in the summer heat after illegally turning on a fire hydrant. The ad reads: "In order to stop young people from turning into criminals we must have one policeman per every five youngsters. People who are willing to turn on a fire hydrant today will most probably be pyromaniacs and flashers tomorrow. . . . If we put all young people in jail today, we will have no criminals tomorrow!"[14] This ad satirically captures the current conditions confronting many young people, especially those at the bottom of the economic ladder. Presumed to be inherently criminal and devious, young people find it difficult to face the future with a sense of hope or possibility.[15] To kids such as these, heroin thus offers an allure different from its romanticized image among past intellectuals and cultural renegades. Music critic Anne Powers succinctly captures a sense of the social malaise many young people feel and details how it fosters a newfound attraction for heroin. She writes:

> In the '90s, far from representing the carelessness of Generation Slack, heroin is surrounded by a strange seriousness—unlike the coke scene, this drug culture advertises its dangers as prominently as its pleasures, with a pessimism that must appeal to young people who have come to expect most satisfactions to carry their own layer of disaster. Its connection to AIDS drives home this message, it's not really possible to be casual, heroin says. It's not really sensible to feel free. . . . As if so many promises—those offered and then betrayed by their ex-hippie parents, those contained within the faltering myth of the consumerist ideal, those seemingly theirs by right of hopeful youth, but poisoned at conception with a divided cynical, polluted world—had left these kids still starving. So they become seduced by the hunger, finding something that offers a way to be driven and aimless at the same time.[16]

Although the reasons behind heroin use among young people are complex, the simple reality is that heroin-related deaths rose significantly in seventeen out of twenty-five major U.S. cities between 1991 and 1994. Moreover, according to Ginna Marston, vice president of the Partnership for a Drug Free America, "Heroin use among . . . 8th-, 10th-, and 12th-graders, is on the increase . . . [and] the number of 12th-graders experimenting with heroin rose from 22,500 in 1991 to 40,000 in 1995."[17] Contributing both to its popularity and the rise in deaths is the fact that heroin has become cheaper and purer.

The issue of heroin chic can be understood and analyzed in both aesthetic and political terms against the contradictory and complex legacy of heroin use as well the changing context of its availability and its increasing use by middle-class professionals and young people. Once heroin chic became an object of national attention, the underlying conditions that produce heroin use and the complicity of fashion advertising and art in legitimating junkie culture became part of a broader public dialogue. Unfortunately, what was missing from this dialogue were serious analyses of the limits that should be respected regarding the connection between art and commerce as well as any public debate about how heroin chic coincided with public attacks on young people—especially minority and working-class youth—who are increasingly seen as the source of society's social problems.

THE PUBLIC POLITICS OF HEROIN CHIC

You do not need to glamorize addiction to sell clothes.
—President Bill Clinton, May 21, 1997

On May 20, 1997, the *New York Times* ran a front-page story on the heroin-related death of twenty-year-old fashion photographer Davide Sorrenti. The article also rebuked fashion magazine editors and photographers for glamorizing what it called the "strung-out heroin addict's look," and it charged that Sorrenti's death reflected widespread heroin use among young people working in the fashion industry. In effect, the article charged that the fashion industry not only glamorized heroin use as an advertising gimmick but was also complicitous with, if not responsible for, promoting and condoning the drug's use within its own ranks.

The following day in a speech before thirty-five mayors from across the United States, President Clinton made "heroin chic" a household phrase by criticizing the fashion industry for glamorizing heroin use. Clinton asserted that fashion photography had sent the wrong message to the American public by making heroin appear "glamorous, sexy, and cool." More to the point, the president raised questions about the role that art plays in shaping public opinion and the degree to which it must take responsibility for the consequences of its actions. Clinton challenged the assumption that the convergence of art and commerce can be understood exclusively in either the language of aesthetics or the language of profit margins. Accusing the fashion industry of being politically and morally remiss, Clinton made clear that it had overstepped its freedoms and exercised its power in a way that was unethical and destructive. He summed up his critique by reminding the fashion industry that "The glorification of heroin is not creative, it's destructive. It's not beautiful, it's ugly. And this is not about art, it's about life and death."[18] What Clinton failed to mention was the role his own administration played in expanding poverty, unemployment, and race-based assaults on many young people through the dismantling of welfare services and the passing of repressively harsh laws that criminalize and unfairly target poor, young, black men.

The photography Clinton referred to had appeared in a wide range of fashion magazines, television ads, and runway shows in the preceding few years.[19] But the heroin chic aesthetic became a dominant part of the cultural landscape not because of its emergence in cutting-edge fashion magazines such as *Detour, W, I-D*, and *The Face* but because Calvin Klein popularized the look in his advertising campaigns, especially his "just be" campaign for "ck be" cologne, which he launched in August 1996. Marking a particularly important moment in the history of heroin chic, "ck be" not only pushed the look into mainstream advertising, it also prompted a public outcry from a number of antidrug groups around the country, much of which went unreported and unnoticed. Klein's "ck be" ads featured black-and-white images of blank-eyed models affecting the languid, sickly expressions of "junk culture" teens waiting outside of a methadone clinic for their next fix. Inserted amid the images appeared a tidy summation— "be this. be that. just be."— suggesting if not glamorizing the tragically hip posturing of the impoverished heroin junkie. "Just be" seemed to offer an ironic alternative to a variety of ad campaigns: from the ultra-patriotic "Be All That You Can Be" army slogan, the ultra-jock "Just Do It" Nike slogan, to the insipid and moralizing "Just say no" slogan that was at the heart of the antidrug campaigns launched during the Reagan era. In response to the latter, "just be" suggested junk culture was not dangerous but fashionable and hip. The ads prompted angry and immediate protest, with a coalition of parent-led antidrug groups leading the charge with the call for a national boycott of Klein's products. Paula Kemp, the associate director of National Families in Action, called upon "Klein's competitors to join the organization in refusing to glamorize addiction in any of their ads."[20] Klein's immediate response to the controversy was typical. Company executives representing Klein argued that they were selling products, not drugs, and that the kids in the ads were "based on real people and the emotions described by those people based on their lives."[21] Clearly, before the high-profile pressure of the White House, Klein's competitors exhibited no concern about the use of heroin chic to sell their products; in fact, many embraced the aesthetic as part of a major marketing strategy.

Fashion photography in the mid-1990s led the way in pushing the heroin chic style to its extreme. A number of young and talented photographers such as Corrine Day, Juergen Teller, Craig McDean, David Sims, Terry Richardson, Steven Meisel, and Mario Sorrenti became more popular because their work emulated the "new realism" that characterized heroin chic. For many of these photographers, what became known as the heroin chic look was in fact their attempt to provide an alternative to the idealized, near-perfect images of beauty and glamour appearing in magazines such as *Harper's Bazaar* or *Vogue*. For instance, Corrine Day's fashion photos in *The Face* often consisted of young kids sitting in chairs or sprawled out on secondhand couches in seedy rooms amid a clutter of empty soda cans, cigarettes, and crumpled newspapers.[22] Day justified her work by claiming it was a reaction against air-brushed, fantasylike images of men and women that served to undermine the truth of people's lives.[23] Steven Meisel's photos of young males dressed in their underwear, sporting tattoos and black nail polish in seedy wood-paneled basements marketed representations of the underclass as a counteraesthetic to idealized notions of beauty. These ads appeared in Calvin Klein's famous 1995 advertising campaign for jeans. Meisel's aesthetic suggests images of "white-trash" kids on the make, selling their bodies for money in cheap trailer park settings. Davide Sorrenti's photos in *Detour* and *I-D* magazines, which appeared in the *New York Times* shortly after his death, include one of model James King looking emaciated, disheveled, and hung over, sitting on a couch surrounded by posters of Sid Vicious and Kurt Cobain. In the January 1997 issue of *W*, a gaunt, sullen model drenched in sweat sits huddled in a chair, an arm extending toward the camera. Commenting on the image, *Boston Globe* reporter Pamela Reynolds pointed out that "the only thing missing was the needle."[24] In many of these designer fashion photos, kids appear with eyes rimmed in dark eye shadow, sprawled on bathroom floors, across disheveled hotel-type beds, and in a variety of shabby and compromising settings.

The fashion industry's response to the charge that its use of heroin chic circulates an image of drug use as vogue and trendy appears, with few exceptions, largely disingenuous. For instance, Calvin Klein, appearing on the June 29, 1997 *Larry King Live* show, simply dismissed the charge by claiming that as a fashion statement, "heroin chic" is both "old-fashioned" and no longer has any credibility. Ignoring the ethical and political implications of such ads, Klein claimed that he was simply selling products. King, always an accommodating host to the rich and famous, allowed Klein's bogus claim to go unchallenged. Terry Jones, an editor of *I-D* magazine, which pioneered the druggy look, responded by claiming that he did not think that heroin chic as a style ever existed. Long Nguyen, style director at *Detour* magazine, claimed such images simply represented a window on life, echoing a defense used by a number of other fashion photographers.[25] In some cases, fashion editors and photographers alike defended the "realism" argument by invoking the photo-documentary work of Nan Goldin, Larry Clark, and Jim Goldberg. Laura Craik, fashion feature editor of *The Face* magazine, invoked another position representative of the fashion world's response to Clinton's speech. She argued that the fashion industry may seduce but it does not peddle drugs. For Craik, it is the working-class pushers and drug runners who bear the responsibility for the appeal of heroin among young people (a not-too-subtle form of racism that pathologizes urban, working-class whites and kids of color).[26]

Each of these defenses deserves a response. First, the work of Goldin, Clark, and Goldberg chronicles particular communities that shaped the lives of the artists. In projects that combine narratives of personal experience, cultural specificity, memories, and historical contexts, each artist uses photography to register how the temporal, personal, and political connect to reveal the "dangerous memories" that mark the social character of communities in which they have lived and which, in part, shaped their own perceptions of society. Moreover, such work is usually accompanied by texts that attempt to construct the viewer not as a distanced voyeur or consumer, as does much photography utilizing the heroin chic motif, but as a moral witness. Both Goldin's narrations of her own experiences of drug abuse and physical battery and Goldberg's moving images of drugged-out, homeless teens do not appropriate the "other" in order to sell commodities in fashion magazines; nor do they make a claim to a specious realism that denies its own political and ideological ramifications as a form of argument, disputation, and way of making the world intelligible.[27]

Unlike much of the fashion photography that is associated with heroin chic, Goldin's and Goldberg's photographs depict the reality of pain and suffering experienced by those who have neither the resources to buy high-end fashion magazines and the clothes they advertise nor the ability to fight back against the objectification of their lives in such magazines. The work of both artists strongly resists the reifying posture of heroin chic photography and grapples with important considerations regarding how "reality and truth are constructed, both aesthetically and socially, in specific historical contexts."[28] Both artists construct images of the "other" within an ideological framework that integrates aesthetic and ethical sensibilities.

If Goldin and Goldberg attempt to reposition social violence in the collective consciousness as a disturbing pathology that undermines public life, the heroin chic crowd reduces representations of human suffering to a privatized, trendy aesthetic that defines the living present outside of a context of struggle, passion, and hope. Art in this case does not evoke violence, death, or human suffering as part of a strategy of moral witnessing and social engagement but crudely represents it as simply more images linking desire and agency exclusively to consumerism. Within the postmodern world of heroin chic fashion photography, the "Other" is an object of aesthetic consideration, a source of sensations rather than a serious object of moral evaluation and responsibility.[29] Realities melt into representations; aesthetic criteria replace considerations of history, politics, power, and morality. A chilling indifference to the experiences of human suffering allows moral apathy and cruelty to become centrally defining principles of artistic production and cultural work. Similarly, the meeting of art and commerce does not deny the political sphere; it simply appropriates that sphere by producing a notion of society and social life that exists in harmony with the reductionistic, reifying demands of the market. Heroin chic may be "old fashioned," but the political and economic forces that legitimate it—forces hardly mentioned by former President Clinton—are still in place. Similarly, the tragic conditions that heroin chic chose to mimic are hardly endemic to the fashion industry; rather they seem to be gaining ground throughout society.

Second, the argument that heroin chic photography in and of itself is wrongly accused of peddling drugs is not without merit. The drug industry cannot be understood outside of a complex set of institutional, political, and ideological relations of power. But in this society the media, including the fashion industry, are crucial in shaping meaning, desire, and identity, especially among young people. Culture matters in both political and educational terms. Politically, those who have the power to control the dominant machineries of cultural production set limits on what can be produced, legitimated, and distributed in a society even as they disproportionately control the conditions under which knowledge becomes accessible to specific groups and individuals. Educationally, the culture industry plays a crucial role in shaping public memory, in legitimating particular ways of knowing and specific forms of knowledge, and in producing identities and the discussions that inform them. By legitimating particular forms of identity and identification, the fashion industry and other cultural spheres play an important, although far from strictly deterministic role in shaping "how we get to know what we know and the moral life we aspire to lead."[30] The fashion industry is not responsible for causing heroin addiction among young people in this country, but it is politically and morally responsible for legitimating the culture of addiction as a vehicle for selling a lifestyle. At the same time, it is culpable for legitimating a type of moral insensitivity that has become widespread, in which images of the poor, oppressed, and disadvantaged are reified, rather than understood as victims or resisters of an often cruel and exploitative social system. Similarly, the fashion industry should be roundly condemned for failing to provide antidrug programs for those who work within its own ranks—such programs are well established in the music and film industries. Educationally, the fashion industry appears to mirror in its own ranks the heroin chic lifestyle it sought to legitimate to a larger public culture; this suggests that rather than merely reflecting the larger society, it actually sought to play a role in constructing values and ideologies that shape social identities.

Confusing the reality of human suffering with an aesthetic that celebrates a politics of despair and pathology, heroin chic does more than generate images in which the lure of cheap sensation is tied to fast money and quick notoriety. Heroin chic also bespeaks a privatized space where art and commerce can withdraw to shield themselves and their viewers from any sense of public accountability. "Heroin chic" must be engaged in more general terms as symptomatic of a market-driven culture that encourages the larger society to view young people as symbols of social degeneracy while simultaneously treating them as both disposable and as an industrial reserve army of consumers. Heroin chic celebrates a society that mocks the poor, increasingly incarcerates its youth, and wages war against people of color. Its brief rise to prominence signals a broader, retrograde public discourse that shares its mocking indifference and celebrates its debased appropriation of the "Other" as an amusing spectacle. Heroin chic offers a postmodern form of cultural slumming as cheap titillation for its yuppie audience, whose members imagine themselves being reckless and edgy as they appropriate the behaviors, dress, modes of speaking, and experiences of those who occupy the most tragic margins of society.

THREE

Kids for Sale: Corporate Culture and the Challenge of Public Schooling

> School is . . . the ideal time to influence attitudes, build
> long-term loyalties, introduce new products, test mar-
> kets, promote sampling and trial usage and—above
> all—to generate immediate sales.
>
> —Cited in Consumer Union Education Services,
> *Captive Kids: Commercial Pressures on Kids at Schools*

PREPARING CITIZENS OR CONSUMERS

One of the most important legacies of American public education
has been providing students with the critical capacities, knowledge,
and values that enable them to become active citizens striving to
build a stronger democratic society. Within this tradition, Americans have defined schooling as a public good and a fundamental
right.[1] Such a definition rightfully asserts the primacy of democratic
values over corporate culture and commercial values. Schools are
an important indicator of the well-being of a democratic society.
They remind us of the civic values that must be passed on to young
people in order for them to think critically, to participate in power

relations and policy decisions that affect their lives, and to transform the racial, social, and economic inequities that limit democratic social relations. Yet as crucial as the role of public schooling has been in American history, it is facing an unprecedented attack from proponents of market ideology who strongly advocate the unparalleled expansion of corporate culture.[2]

Influential educational consultants such as Robert Zemsky of Stanford University and Chester Finn of the Hudson Institute now "advise their clients in the name of efficiency to act like corporations selling products and seek 'market niches' to save themselves." They are advised to adopt such strategies so to meet the challenges of the new world economic order.[3] School leaders are now drawn from the ranks of corporate executives, employing a managerial style that describes school systems as "major companies," students as "customers," and learning as a measurable outcome. One example of the new corporate school leader was highlighted in a recent article in The New York Times. Under the byline, "Applying Corporate Touch to a Troubled School System," the article focuses on Andre J. Hornsby, the new superintendent of the Yonkers school district, the fourth largest in New York City. Touted as a model for the type of leadership now in vogue among urban schools systems, the Times describes him as "arrogant, autocratic, an egomaniac . . . adamant that poor minority children can overcome their socioeconomic hurdles, driven to raise scores on standardized tests using cookie-cutter curriculums, and assuming an almost militaristic take-charge approach." Without skipping a beat the article then goes on to point out that one of Mr. Hornsby's first initiatives was to impose additional work loads on his teachers, which prompted a strike, and at his initiative prompted a successful court battle to prevent extra resources from being distributed to "eight school districts the courts identified as being in most need." It seems that in spite of Mr. Hornsby's concern for poor students, he preferred to distribute the extra money among all school districts, "a tactic favored by the predominantly white school board that hired him."[4] Hornsby appears typical of a corporate leadership model that has nothing to say about inequality, wields power autocratically, reduces curricula to the language of standards and testing, and makes sure that teachers have little control over the conditions of teaching and learning.

The advocates of corporate culture no longer view public education in terms of its civic function; rather it is primarily a commercial venture in which the only form of citizenship available for young people is consumerism. In what follows, I argue that reducing public education to the ideological imperatives of the corporate order works against the critical social demands of educating citizens to sustain and develop inclusive democratic identities, relations, and public spheres. Underlying this analysis is the assumption that the struggle to reclaim the public schools must be seen as part of a broader battle over the defense of children's culture and the public good. At the heart of such a struggle is the need to challenge the ever-growing influence of corporate power and politics.

The corporatizing of public education has taken a distinct turn as we approach the twenty-first century. No longer content merely to argue for the application of business principles to the organization of schooling, the forces of corporate culture have adopted a much more radical agenda. Central to this agenda is the attempt to transform public education from a public good, benefiting all students, to a private good designed to expand the profits of investors, educate students as consumers, and train young people for the low-paying jobs of the new global marketplace. And the stakes are high. According to the *Education Industry Directory*, the for-profit education market represents $600 billion in revenue for corporate interests.[5] And this is an expanding market, "larger than either the military budget or social security."[6] The lure of such big profits has attracted a range of investors including former junk bond wizard Michael Milken along with an increasing number of corporate players such as Apple, Sony, Microsoft, Oracle, and the *Washington Post*.[7]

But the corporate takeover of schools is not rationalized in the name of profits and market efficiency alone, it is also legitimated through the call for vouchers, privatized choice plans, and excellence. Although this discourse cloaks itself in the democratic principles of freedom, individualism, and consumer rights, it fails to provide the broader historical, social, and political contexts necessary to render such principles meaningful and applicable, particularly with respect to the problems facing public schools.

While a wide range of marketplace-based approaches to schooling exist, all share a faith in corporate culture that overrides defending public education as a noncommodified public sphere, a repository for nourishing the primacy of civic over corporate values, and as a public entitlement that is essential for the well-being of children and the future of democracy.

THE POLITICS OF PRIVATIZATION

Privatization is the most powerful educational reform movement to come since the *Sputnik* crisis caused a panic among educators in the 1950s when schools rushed to prepare a new generation of scientists to lead the American space race against the Russians. The movement is funded by an array of conservative institutions such as the Heritage Foundation, the Hudson Institute, and the Olin Foundation.[8] Capitalizing on their wealth and media influence, these foundations have enlisted an army of conservative pundits, many of whom served in the Department of Education under Presidents Reagan and Bush. Some of the better-known members of this reform movement include Chester Finn, Jr., Lamar Alexander, Diane Ravitch, David Kearns, and William Bennett. Providing policy papers and op-ed commentaries, appearing on television talk shows, and running a variety of educational clearinghouses and resource centers, these stalwart opponents of public education relentlessly blame the schools for the country's economic woes. Diane Ravitch and others cite low test scores, a decline in basic skills, and the watering down of the school curriculum in order to legitimate the ideology of privatization with its accompanying call for vouchers, privatized charter schools, and the placing of public schools entirely under the control of corporate contractors.[9] More specific reforms simply recycle right-wing ideology critiques calling for the replacement of teacher unions and "giving parents choice, back-to-basics and performance-driven curriculums, management 'design teams' and accountability."[10]

Underlying the call for privatization is a reform movement in which public education is seen as "a local industry that over time will become a global business."[11] As a for-profit venture, public education represents a rapidly growing market and a lucrative source of profits. The importance of such a market has not been lost on conservatives such as Chester Finn, Jr. and David Kearns, both of whom have connections with for-profit schooling groups such as the Edison Project and the North American Schools Development Corporation respectfully. At the level of policy, by all reports the right-wing assault has been quite successful. More than twenty-eight states have drafted legislation supporting vouchers, choice programs, and contracting with for-profit management companies, such as the Edison Project and Sabis International Schools. But the public's perception of such ventures appears to be less enthusiastic, and rightly so. Many firms, such as Educational Alternatives Inc., which took over the Hartford and Baltimore public schools, have had their contracts canceled as a result of numerous public complaints. The complaints range from the way in which such firms deal with children with learning disabilities and engage in union busting to the charge that their cookie-cutter standardized curriculum and testing packages fail to provide the quality of educational results that such companies initially promised.[12]

But there is more at stake in the privatization of public schooling than issues of public versus private ownership or public good versus private gain. There is also the issue of how individual achievement is weighed against issues of equity and the social good, how teaching and learning are defined, and what sorts of identities are produced when the histories, experiences, values, and desires of students are delineated through corporate rather than democratic ideals.

Within the language of privatization and market reforms, there is a strong emphasis on standards, measurements of outcomes, and holding teachers and students more accountable. Privatization is an appealing prospect for legislators who do not want to spend money on schools and for those Americans who feel that they do not want to support public education through increased taxes. Such appeals are reductive in nature and hollow in substance. Not only do they remove questions of equity and equality from the discussion of standards, they appropriate the democratic rhetoric of choice and freedom without addressing issues of power. In their refusal to address the financial inequities that burden the public schools, the ideas and images that permeate this corporate model of schooling reek with the rhetoric of insincerity and the politics of social indifference. Educational theorist Jonathan Kozol captures this sentiment well. He writes:

> To speak of national standards and, increasingly, of national exams but never to dare speak of national equality is a transparent venture into punitive hypocrisy. Thus, the children in poor rural schools in Mississippi and Ohio will continue to get education funded at less than $4,000 yearly and children in the South Bronx will get less than $7,000, while children in the richest suburbs will continue to receive up to $18,000 yearly. But they'll all be told they must be held to the same standards and they'll all be judged, of course, by their performance on the same exams.[13]

Because they have no language of social responsibility, the advocates of privatization reject the assumption that school failure might be better understood within the political, economic, and social dynamics of poverty, joblessness, sexism, race and class discrimination, unequal funding, or a diminished tax base. Rather, student failure, especially the failure of poor minority-group students, often is attributed to a genetically encoded lack of intelligence, a culture of deprivation, or simply to pathology. Books such as *The Bell Curve*[14] and films such as *Dangerous Minds* and *187* reinforce such representations of African American and Latino urban youth and in doing so reinforce and perpetuate a legacy of racist exclusions. Similarly, the informalities of privatization schemes in which schools simply mimic the free market, with the assumption that its regulatory and competitive spirit will allow the most motivated and gifted students to succeed, deepen such racist exclusions. A shameful element of racism and a retrograde social Darwinism permeates this attitude, one that relinquishes the responsibility of parents, teachers, administrators, social workers, businesspeople, and other members of the wider society to provide *all* young people with the cultural resources, economic opportunities, and social services necessary to learn without having to bear the crushing burdens of poverty, racism, and other forms of oppression.

The excessive celebration by privatization's advocates of an individual's sovereign interests does more than remove the dynamics of student performance from broader social and political considerations; it also feeds a value system in which compassion, solidarity, cooperation, social responsibility, and other attributes of education as a social good get displaced by defining education exclusively as a private good. If education is about, in part, creating particular identities, what dominates the corporate model is a notion of the student as an individual consumer and teachers as the ultimate salespeople.[15] Education scholar David Labaree is right in arguing that such an educational model undermines the traditional notion that education is a public good that should benefit all children and must be viewed as central to the democratic health of a society. But when viewed as a private good whose organizing principle is simply to mimic the market, education as the experience of democracy is transformed into a discourse and ideology of privilege driven by narrow individual interests. Labaree is quite clear on this issue:

> In an educational system where the consumer is king . . . education . . . is a private good that only benefits the owner, an investment in my future, not yours, in my children, not other people's children. For such an educational system to work effectively, it needs to focus a lot of attention on grading, sorting, and selecting students. It needs to provide a variety of ways for individuals to distinguish themselves from others—such as by placing themselves in a more prestigious college, a higher curriculum track, the top reading group, or the gifted program.[16]

In this framework education becomes less a social investment than an individual investment, a vehicle for social mobility for those privileged to have the resources and power to make their choices matter, and a form of social constraint for those who lack such resources and for whom choice and accountability betray a legacy of broken promises and an ideology of bad faith.

The privatization model of schooling also undermines the power of teachers to provide students with the vocabulary and skills of critical citizenship. Under the drive to impose national curricula uniformity and standardized testing, privatizing school advocates devalue teacher authority and subvert teacher skills by dictating not only what they teach but also how they should teach. California, for example, is drafting legislation that mandates both the content of school knowledge and "more specific guidelines for when and how to teach various principles in the core subjects."[17]

In this perspective teaching is completely removed from the cultural and social contexts that shape particular traditions, histories, and experiences in a community and school. Hence, this model of educational reform fails to recognize that students come from different backgrounds, bring diverse cultural experiences with them to the classroom, and relate to the world in different ways. Importance is no longer placed on having teachers begin with those places, histories, and experiences that actually constitute students' lives in order to connect whatever knowledge they learn to existing frameworks of reference. Rather, teaching in the corporate model translates educational exchange into financial exchange, critical learning into mastery, and leadership into management. This perspective lacks the ability to acknowledge students' histories, the stories that inform their lives, and the educational imperative of weaving such information into webs of meaning that link the everyday with the academic. Corporate education opposes such a critical approach because it cannot be standardized, routinized, and reduced to a prepackaged curriculum; on the contrary, a critical and transformative educational practice takes seriously the abilities of teachers to theorize, contextualize, and honor their students' diverse lives. It is far removed from a corporate educational system based on an industrial model of learning that represents a flagrant violation of the democratic educational mission.

A debilitating logic is at work in the corporate model of teaching with its mandated curriculum, top-down teaching practices, and national tests to measure educational standards. Infused with the drive toward standardized curricula and teaching, "teachers and communities shorn of the capacity to use their own ideas, judgments, and initiative in matters of importance can't teach kids to do so."[18] Such approaches have little to do with teaching students to develop critical skills and an awareness of the operations of power that would enable them to both locate themselves in the world and to intervene in and shape it effectively.[19] On the contrary, corporate educational policies undermine such critical approaches by defining teaching less as an intellectual activity and more as a standardized, mechanical, and utterly passive mode of transmission. Sociologist Stanley Aronowitz argues that such a system largely functions to "measure" student progress while simultaneously reproducing a tracking system that parallels the deep racial and economic inequalities of the larger society. He writes:

> Where once liberal, let alone radical, educators insisted that education be at the core an activity of self-exploration in which,

through intellectual and affective encounters, the student attempts to discover her own subjectivity, now nearly all learning space is occupied by an elaborate testing apparatus that measures the student's "progress" in ingesting externally imposed curricula and, more insidiously, provides a sorting device to reproduce the inequalities inherent in the capitalist market system.[20]

The main role of the teacher-turned-classroom manager is to legitimate through mandated subject matter and educational practices a market-based conception of the learner as simply a consumer of information. Yet such reforms have support, in spite of a long tradition of critique of the ways in which teachers are being shorn of their skills and increasingly treated "more and more as impersonal instruments in a bureaucratic process than as thoughtful and creative intellectuals whose personal vision of education really matters."[21] Moreover, within the standardized teaching models proffered by corporations, it is difficult to offer students the opportunity to think critically about the knowledge they gain, to appreciate the value of learning as more than the mastery of discrete bits of information, or how to use knowledge as a form of power to fight injustices in a market-based society founded on deep inequalities of power. Given the vested interests that conglomerates have in turning students "into consumers and avenues to a vast consumer base," it is highly improbable that schools will be allowed to foster resistance to corporate ideologies. And this fact becomes increasingly more likely as corporations control publishing companies, magazines, newspapers, and other knowledge-producing sources. For example, *New York Times* writer Russell Baker writing about Michael Milken's foray into for-profit education speculates about whether a Milken School would allow teachers and students to critically examine the financial corruption that marked a number of business scandals in the 1980s, including the way in which Milken used his power as a junk bond dealer and financial adviser to downsize companies and eventually throw thousands of people out of work. In response to such an inquiry, Baker writes that a former colleague says "'Absolutely not.'" He concludes that "Such concerns seem borne out in a book produced by a Milken-backed publishing house, Knowledge Exchange. Its *Business Encyclopedia* approvingly cites Milken's role in the junk-bond market without mention of the economic and social devastation associated with it."[22]

One could raise the censorship issue about a number of corporations that have made heavy investments in gaining a share of the education market. For example, Disney has been criticized in a number of quarters for preventing critical news commentators and stories from being aired on its radio stations.[23] In light of such allegations, it is conceivable that Disney would exercise the same type of censorship on curricular materials used in the schools that were critical of, let us say, its outsourcing of the production of its clothing and toys to sweatshops in such countries as Haiti, Burma, Vietnam, and China.[24] In addition, if such conglomerates can slash "surplus teachers" in order to become more cost effective, they can easily legitimate and select teaching materials that contribute positively to their public relations campaigns.

Finally, it is no small matter that the project that fuels privatization not only celebrates competitive, self-interested individuals attempting to further their own needs and aspirations but also takes place within a dialogue of decline, a jeremiad against public life. In doing so it actually undermines the role that public schools might play in keeping the experiences, hopes, and dreams of a democracy alive for each successive generation of students.

The major objective of privatization is that public schools conform to the needs of the market and reflect more completely the interests of corporate culture—in essence, the private sector should control and own the public schools. While this represents the most direct assault on schooling as a public sphere, the program does not stop there. A different but no less important and dangerous strategy of the corporate dismantling and takeover of public schools is the promotion of educational choice, vouchers, and charters as a way of both opening public schools to private contractors and using public tax monies to finance private forms of education. Both approaches treat education as a private good, and both transform the student's role from citizen to educational consumer. But the real danger at work in privatization, as educational theorist Jeffrey Henig points out, is not simply that students who transfer into private schools will drain money from the public schools but that they will further a process already at work in the larger society aimed at eroding "the public forums in which decisions with social consequences can be democratically resolved."[25]

COMMERCIALIZATION IN SCHOOLS

Corporate culture can be seen not only in the placement of public schools in the control of corporate contractors. It is also visible in the growing commercialization of school space and curricula. Strapped for money, many public schools have had to lease out space in their hallways, buses, rest rooms, monthly lunch menus, and school cafeterias, transforming such spaces into glittering billboards for the highest corporate bidder.[26] School notices, classroom displays, and student artwork have been replaced by advertisements for Coca-Cola, Pepsi, Nike, Hollywood films, and a litany of other products. Invaded by candy manufacturers, breakfast cereal makers, sneaker companies, and fast food chains, schools increasingly offer the not-so-subtle message to students that everything is for sale including student identities, desires, and values. Seduced by the lure of free equipment and money, schools all too readily make the transition from advertising to offering commercial merchandise in the form of curricula materials designed to build brand loyalty and markets among a captive public school audience. Although schools may reap small financial benefit from such school-business transactions, the real profits go to the corporations that spend millions on advertising to reach a market of an estimated 43 million children in school "with spending power of over \$108 billion per year and the power to influence parental spending."[27]

The commercial logic that fuels this market-based reform movement is also evident in the way in which corporate culture targets schools not simply as investments for substantial profits but also as training grounds for educating students to define themselves as consumers rather than as multifaceted social actors. As schools struggle to raise money for texts, curricula, and extracurricular activities, they engage in partnerships with businesses that are all too willing to provide free curriculum packages; as in the case of companies such as Channel One that provide each school with \$50,000 in "free" electronic equipment, including VCRs, televisions, and satellite dishes, on the condition that the schools agree to broadcast a ten-minute program of current events and news material along with two minutes of commercials.[28] A number of companies want to capitalize on cash-poor schools in order to gain a foothold to promote learning as a way to create "consumers in training." For example, ZapMe, a Silicon Valley company, "gives schools free personal computers and Internet access in exchange for the right to display a constant stream of on-screen advertisements. Participating schools must also promise that the system will be in use for at least four hours per school day."[29]

The marriage of commercialism and education often takes place in schools with too few resources to critically monitor how learning is structured or to recognize the sleight-of-hand that appears to be a generous offer on the part of corporations. A few examples will suffice. In a recent cover story, *Business Week* magazine reported on the adoption of a McDonald's-sponsored curriculum package by the Pembroke Lakes elementary school in Broward County, Florida. Commenting on what one ten-year-old learned from the curricula, *Business Week* claimed that "Travis Licate recently learned how to design a McDonald's restaurant, how a McDonald's works, and how to apply and interview for a job at McDonald's thanks to [the] seven-week company-sponsored class intended to teach kids about the work world."[30] When Travis was asked if the curriculum was worthwhile, he responded: "If you want to work in a McDonald's when you grow up, you already know what to do. . . . Also, McDonald's is better than Burger King."[31] According to the Center for Commercial-Free Public Education, Exxon developed a curriculum that teaches young students that the Valdez oil spill was an example of environmental protection. The center also cites a Nike-sponsored curriculum that teaches students to learn how a Nike shoe is created but fails to address "the sweatshop portion of the manufacturing process."[32] McGraw-Hill recently published an elementary-school math textbook full of advertisements for products such as Nike, Gatorade, and Sony PlayStations. Another company offers a math exercise book that "purports to teach third-graders math by having them count Tootsie Rolls."[33] Such curricula have little to do with critical learning and a great deal with producing debased narratives of citizenship, suggesting to students that the only roles open to them are defined through the ethos of consumerism. The version of citizenship presented in this commercial educational system debases public life and privatizes learning by removing it from noncommercial values and considerations.[34]

Many school systems not only accept corporate-sponsored curricula, they also lease out space in their hallways, on their buses, and even on book covers. Cover Concepts Marketing Services, Inc., for example, provides schools with free book covers strategically designed to promote brand-name products that include Nike, Gitano, FootLocker, Starburst, Nestlé, and Pepsi. The covers are distributed to over 8,000 public schools and reach an audience of over 6 million high school, junior high, and elementary school students.[35] In Colorado Springs, Colorado, Palmer High School allows Burger King and Sprite to advertise on the sides of its school buses. In Salt Lake City, Youthtalk Advertising Agency places acrylic-faced advertising billboards in school rest rooms and cafeterias. It is estimated by the company that over "80,000 students are exposed to the ads while standing at urinals and sitting in toilet stalls."[36]

A number of public and private schools are also allowing corporations to harness students as captive audiences for market research during the school day. Trading student time for industry resources, many schools forge partnerships with corporations in which students become the objects of market-based group research. Corporations give the schools money, equipment, or curricula for the right to use students to take taste tests, experiment with different products, or answer opinion polls in which they are asked questions that range from "where they got their news [to] what television shows they like."[37] Some educators eager to justify such blatant acts of commercialism argue that these practices constitute a genuine learning experience for students; in doing so they often appear to be merely echoing the words of research consultants who claim that such market-based approaches are actually empowering for kids. For example, Martha Marie Pooler, the principal of Our Lady of Assumption elementary school in Lynnfield, Massachusetts, agreed to accept $600 for her school in exchange for a corporation using students in a cereal taste test. She justified this type of corporate intrusion by claiming that the test had educational benefits in that it was similar "to conducting a science-class experiment."[38] Pooler is part of a growing number of educators who refuse to face the serious ethical dilemmas involved in allowing companies to conduct market research on children who should be learning critical knowledge and skills that, at the very least, would enable them to refuse to participate in such exploitative behavior. Not only do the students have no say in participating in such market driven tests, they, along with the teachers, appear powerless as the school shifts its priorities from education to marketing products. Andrew Hagelshaw, a senior program director of the Center for Commercial-Free Public Education in Oakland, California rightfully argues that "companies are turning schools into sales agents for their products . . . [and are] going to change the priorities from education to . . . consumption."[39] The National Association of State Boards of Education recently argued that schools that offer captive audiences of children in classrooms as fodder for commercial profit are engaging in practices that constitute both an act of "exploitation and a violation of the public trust."[40] Such violations of the public trust present a major challenge to those educators, parents, and concerned citizens who want to protect children from corporate intrusion into their lives.

Schools are being transformed into commercial rather than public spheres as students become subject to the whims and practices of marketers whose agenda has nothing to do with critical learning and a great deal to do with restructuring civic life in the image of market culture.[41] Civic courage—upholding the most basic non-commercial principles of democracy—as a defining principle of society is devalued as corporate power transforms school knowledge so that students are taught to recognize brand names or learn the appropriate attitudes for future work in low-skilled, low-paying jobs. They are no longer taught how to connect the meaning of work to the imperatives of a strong democracy. What links Channel One, Nike, Pepsi, the Campbell Soup Company, the McDonald Corporation, and a host of others is that they substitute corporate propaganda for real learning, upset the requisite balance between the public and the private, and in doing so treat schools like any other business.

Underlying the attempt to redefine the meaning and purpose of schooling as part of a market economy rather than a fundamental feature of substantive democracy is a model of society in which "consumer accountability [is] mediated by a relationship with an educational market [rather than] a democratic accountability mediated by a relationship with the whole community of citizens."[42] Most disturbing about the market approach to schooling is that it contains no special consideration for the vocabulary of ethics and values. British educator Gerald Grace insightfully argues that when public education becomes a venue for making a profit, delivering a product, or constructing consuming subjects, education reneges on its responsibilities for creating a democracy of citizens by shifting its focus to producing a democracy of consumers.[43]

Growing up corporate has become a way of life for American youth. This is evident as corporate mergers consolidate control of assets and markets, particularly as they extend their influence over the media and its management of public opinion. But it is also apparent in the accelerated commercialism in all aspects of everyday life, including the "commercialization of public schools, the renaming of public streets for commercial sponsors, Janis Joplin's Mercedes pitch, restroom advertising, and [even the marketing] of an official commercial bottled water for a papal visit."[44] Although it is largely recognized that market culture exercises a powerful educational role in mobilizing desires and shaping identities, it still comes as a shock when an increasing number of pollsters report that young people, when asked to provide a definition for democracy, answered by referring to "the freedom to buy and consume whatever they wish, without government restriction."[45]

Couched in the language of business competition and individual success, the current educational reform movement must be recognized as a full-fledged attack on both public education and democracy itself. Social critic David Stratman's warning that the goal of such a movement "is not to raise the expectations of our young people but to narrow, stifle, and crush them"[46] needs to be taken seriously by anyone concerned about public education. This is particularly true if public education is to play a fundamental role in placing limits on market culture, affirming the language of moral compassion, and expanding the meaning of freedom and choice to broader considerations of equity, justice, and social responsibility.

As market culture permeates the social order, it threatens to diminish the tension between market values and democratic values, such as justice; freedom; equality; respect for children; and the rights of citizens as equal, free human beings. Without such values, children are relegated to the role of economic calculating machines, and the growing disregard for public life that appears to be gaining ground in the United States is left unchecked.

History has been clear about the dangers of unbridled corporate power. Four hundred years of slavery; ongoing although unofficial segregation; the exploitation of child labor; the sanctioning of cruel working conditions in coal mines and sweatshops; and the destruction of the environment have all been fueled by the law of maximizing profits and minimizing costs, especially when civil society offers no countervailing power to hold such forces in check. This is not to suggest that corporations are the enemy of democracy but to highlight the importance of a strong democratic civil society that limits the reach and effects of corporate culture.[47] John Dewey correctly argues that democracy requires work, but that work is not synonymous with democracy.[48]

Educational critic Alex Molnar rightfully cautions educators that the market does not provide "guidance on matters of justice and fairness that are at the heart of a democratic civil society."[49] The power of corporate culture, when left to its own devices, respects few boundaries and even fewer basic social needs, such as the need for uncontaminated food, decent health care, and safe forms of transportation. This was made clear, for example, in recent revelations about the failure of tobacco companies to reveal evidence about the addictive nature of nicotine. In direct violation of broader health considerations, these corporations effectively promoted the addiction of young smokers to increase sales and profits. Moreover, as multinational corporations increase their control over the circulation of information in the media, little is mentioned about how they undermine the principles of justice and freedom that should be at the center of our most vital civic institutions. Developing a vocabulary that affirms non-market values such as love, trust, and compassion is particularly important for the public schools, whose function, in part, is to teach students about the importance of critical dialogue, debate, and decision making in a participatory democracy.

One recent incident at a public school in Evans, Georgia, provides an example of how corporate culture actually can be used to punish students who challenge the corporate approach to learning. Greenbrier High School decided to participate in an Education Day as part of a larger district-wide contest sponsored by Coca-Cola executives. Each school that entered the contest sponsored rallies, heard speeches from Coke executives, analyzed the sugar content of Coke in chemistry classes, and gathered for "an aerial photograph of the students' bodies dressed in red and white and forming the word 'coke.' The reward for winning the district-wide contest—five hundred dollars."[50] Two students decided to disrupt the photo shoot by removing their shirts to reveal Pepsi logos. Both students were suspended on the grounds that they were rude. What students learned as a result is that the individual right to dissent, to freely express their opinions and ideas, and to challenge authority, when addressed within the context of commercial culture, is a punishable offense. Choice in this context is about choosing the right soft drink, not about the right to question whether schools should be turned into advertising billboards for corporate interests.

EDUCATION AND THE IMPERATIVES OF DEMOCRACY

Challenging the encroachment of corporate power is essential if democracy is to remain a defining principle of education and everyday life. In order to mobilize such a challenge educators need to create organizations capable of providing an alternative conception of the meaning and purpose of public education, one that links education to expanding and deepening democracy itself. Educators must also create political coalitions that have the power and resources to produce legislation that limits corporate power's ascendancy over the institutions and mechanisms of civil society. This project requires that educators and students provide the rationale and mobilize the possibility for the creation of enclaves of resistance, new public cultures and institutional spaces that highlight, nourish, and evaluate the tension between civil society and corporate power while simultaneously emphasizing citizen rights rather than consumer rights.

Educators, families, and community members need to reinvigorate the language, social relations, and politics of schooling. We must analyze how power shapes knowledge, how teaching broader social values provides safeguards against turning citizenship skills into workplace-training skills, and how schooling can help students reconcile the seemingly opposing needs of freedom and solidarity. As educators, we need to examine alternative models of education that challenge the corporatization of public schools. For example, pioneering educators such Deborah Meier, Ted Sizer, James Comer, and organizations like the Rethinking School Collective, among others, are working hard to link educational policies and classroom practices to expand the scope of freedom, justice, and democracy.

In strategic terms, in order to revitalize public dialogue, educators need to take seriously the importance of defending public education as an institution whose purpose is to educate students for active citizenship.[51] Schooling is a site that offers students the opportunity to be involved in the deepest problems of society and to acquire the knowledge, skills, and ethical vocabulary necessary to actively participate in democratic public life. Educators need to come together locally and nationally to defend public schools as indispensable to the life of the nation because they are one of the few remaining public spheres where students can gain the knowledge and skills they need for learning how to govern, take risks, and develop the knowledge necessary for deliberation, reasoned arguments, and social action. At issue is providing students with an education that allows them to recognize the dream and promise of a substantive democracy, particularly the idea that as citizens, as historian Robin Kelley points out, they are "entitled to public services, decent housing, safety, security, support during hard times, and most importantly, some power over decision making."[52] Social critics Carol Ascher, Norm Fruchter, and Robert Berne capture the gravity of such a project in their claim that the urgency to solve the inequities in schooling is perhaps the most important reason for continuing the struggle to reform public education. For we will not survive as a republic nor move toward a genuine democracy unless we can narrow the gap between the rich and the poor, reduce our racial and ethnic divides, and create a deeper sense of community.[53]

But more is needed than defending public education as central to developing and nourishing the proper balance between democratic public spheres and commercial power, between identities founded on democratic principles and identities steeped in forms of competitive, self-interested individualism that celebrate their own material and ideological advantages. Given the current attempts by state legislators to limit the power educators have over the curriculum and classroom teachers, it is politically crucial that such educators be defended as public intellectuals who provide an indispensable service to the nation. Such an appeal cannot be made merely in the name of disinterested scholarship and professionalism, but in terms of such educators' civic duty to provide students with the knowledge and skills they need to participate in and shape ongoing public conversations about crucial political, social, and cultural issues. Educators in our nation's schools represent the conscience of a society; they shape the conditions under which future generations learn about themselves and their relations to others and the world and they also employ teaching practices that are by their very nature moral and political rather than simply technical. And at their best, such practices bear witness to the ethical and political dilemmas that animate the broader social landscape.

Organizing against the corporate takeover of schools also suggests fighting to protect collective bargaining and health benefits for teachers, developing legislation to prevent untrained teachers from assuming classroom responsibilities, and working to put more power into the hands of faculty, parents, and students. Educators at the public school level are under massive assault in this country. Not only are they increasingly losing their autonomy and capacity for imaginative teaching, they bear the burden, especially in the urban centers, of overcrowded classes, limited resources, and hostile legislators. Such educators need to form alliances with parents, social movements, and progressive legislators around a common platform that resists the corporatizing of schools, reducing teachers' skills, and limiting learning to the narrow dictates of efficiency and standardization. Local and national committees can be organized to protect public schools from becoming subject to the whims and interests of corporations. Such organizations can put pressure on legislators to pass laws to ban commercial logos and brand name advertisements on school property, including in books, on the walls of schools, and on the sides of buses. Steve Manning highlights the role that parents in Seattle played in organizing against the commercialization of the public schools. He writes:

> In Seattle, parents organized a series of "commercialism walk-throughs" of the city's schools, collecting as many examples of commercial material as they could. Their findings helped to stop a proposed district wide policy that would have allowed corporate advertising in schools, and led to the formation of a school/community task force to study the issue.[54]

Such actions need to be publicized and links need to be developed between parents and social movements around the country who can learn from each other how to stop such commercialization from shaping school policies.

The growing corporate influence on American education reflects a crisis of vision regarding the meaning and purpose of democracy at a time when "market cultures, market moralities, market mentalities [are] shattering community, eroding civic society, [and] undermining the nurturing system for children."[55] Yet such a crisis also represents a unique opportunity for progressive educators to reaffirm the meaning and importance of democracy—radically defined as a struggle to combine the distribution of wealth, income, and knowledge with a recognition and positive valuation of cultural diversity—by reasserting the primacy of politics, power, and struggle as an educational task. Educators need to confront the march of corporate power by resurrecting a noble tradition, extending from Horace Mann to Martin Luther King, Jr., in which education is affirmed as a political process that encourages people to identify themselves as more than consuming subjects and democracy as more than a spectacle of market culture. Evidence of such struggles can be seen in school districts across the country where students, parents, and community activists are fighting against the commercialization of schools. Steven Manning of the Open Society Institute in New York reports that student activist Sarah Church led a successful campaign to prevent Pepsi-Cola from contracting an exclusive vending deal with Berkeley High School in exchange for a $90,000 electronic scoreboard for the football stadium. He also highlights the passing of the Commercial Free Schools Act by the San Francisco School Board. As he points out, the "act bars the district from signing exclusive beverage contracts or adopting educational materials that contain brand names."[56]

Finally, it is worth remembering that the debate about public education is really about what form the relationship between corporations and public life is going to take in the next century. The meaning and purpose of such a debate has not been lost on students. During the first week of March 1998, students from over 100 colleges held a series of "teach-ins" protesting the intrusion and increasing involvement of corporations in public and higher education.[57] For those who work in such institutions as well as for those concerned about the plight of children in this country, it is time to provide an example through our own actions of the meaning and importance of civic courage.

CULTURAL POLITICS
AND PUBLIC PEDAGOGY

FOUR

Radical Education and Culture in the Work of Antonio Gramsci

INTRODUCTION

Sixty years after his death, Antonio Gramsci still looms large as one of the great political theorists of the twentieth century. Born in Sardinia in 1891, Gramsci eventually settled in the industrial city of Turin in Northern Italy. After splitting from the socialist party, he founded the Italian Communist Party, which he headed from 1924 until he was imprisoned by Mussolini's fascist regime in 1926. During his trial for crimes against the state, the government prosecutor argued that "We must stop this brain from functioning for twenty years." Gramsci died in 1937, the day after he was released. During the time he was imprisoned, he wrote endlessly on culture and politics, though in a cryptic style in order to evade prison censors. Eventually his notes were smuggled out of prison and published. Soon afterwards, he was recognized as one of the major figures of Western Marxism, especially for his work on culture, civil society, education, and hegemony as a form of cultural and social leadership. Refusing to separate culture from systemic relations of power, or politics from the production of knowledge and identities, Gramsci redefined how politics influences everyday life through the force of its educational practices, relations, and discourses. This position is in stark contrast to a growing and insistent number of contemporary progressive theorists who remove politics from culture and political struggle from educational practices. Unlike Gramsci, such theorists emphasize a materialist politics that ignores the ways in which cultural formations have become one of the chief means through which individuals engage and comprehend the material circumstances and forces that shape their lives. In a strange twist of politics, many progressives and left intellectuals now view culture as ornamental, a burden on class-based politics, or identical with a much-maligned identity politics.[1]

Gramsci's work both challenges this position and provides a theoretical framework for understanding how class is always lived through the modalities of race and gender.[2] Moreover, Gramsci's work provides an important political corrective to those social theories that fail to acknowledge how educational politics work in shaping and articulating the divide between diverse institutional and cultural formations. For Gramsci, social theory at its best expands the meaning of the political by being self-conscious about the way education works through its own cultural practices. Education works in such a way so as to legitimate its motivating questions, secure particular modes of authority, and give priority to particular "institutional frameworks and disciplinary rules by which its research imperatives are formed."[3]

According to Gramsci, culture had to be addressed as part of a new political configuration and set of historical conditions that emerged in the beginning of the twentieth century in the advanced industrial societies of the West. Intellectuals could not address the institutional arrangements of capitalism and the changing politics of class formation without being attentive to how common sense and consent were being constructed within public spheres marked by the emergence of new technologies and specific, yet shifting educational practices. Such an understanding required not only a

new attentiveness to "culture in its political role and consequences"[4] but emphasized the issue of how alternative cultural
spheres might be transformed into sites of struggle and resistance
animated by a new group of intellectuals.

While the context in which we now read Gramsci's work is
radically different from the historical context in which his politics
and theories developed, Gramsci's views on the relationship among
culture, education, and power provide an important theoretical
resource for addressing the challenges currently facing public and
higher education in the United States. Here I analyze the importance
of Gramsci's work, especially his work on education, by first outlining
the nature of the current right-wing attempt to subordinate public
and higher education to the needs of capital—substituting the
purpose and meaning of education from a public to a private good—
and the central role that cultural politics plays in spearheading such
an assault. In addition, I examine the attempt of right-wing theorists
such as E. D. Hirsch, Jr. to appropriate Gramsci's views on education
for a conservative educational project. Finally, I conclude by analyzing the implications that Gramsci's work might have for defending
education as a public good and for positioning cultural pedagogy as
central to any discourse of radical politics.

DEMOCRACY AND EDUCATION UNDER SIEGE

As the world moves into the next millennium, questions of culture
have become central to understanding how politics and power
reorganize the social and economic forces that profoundly effect
and regulate everyday life. The politics of culture can be seen not
only in the ways that symbolic resources and knowledge have
replaced traditional skills as society's primary productive force but
also in the role that culture now plays as the main educational force
that secures the authority and interests of dominant groups. Media
technologies have redefined the power of particular groups to
construct a representational politics that plays a crucial role in

shaping self and group identities as well as determining and marking off different conceptions of community and belonging. The notion that culture has become an important site of contestation and tool of power has not been lost on conservatives and the growing forces of the new right.[5]

Beginning with Ronald Reagan and George Bush in the 1980s and culminating with the Newt Gingrich Republican revolution of the 1990s, conservatives have taken control of an ever-growing electronic media industry and a new global communication systems—demonstrating that politics has taken on an important educational function in the information age.[6] Recognizing the political value of defining culture as both a site of struggle and a sphere of education becomes central to social and political change. Conservatives have easily outmaneuvered progressives in the ongoing battle over control of the production of knowledge, values, identities, desires, and those social practices central to winning the consent of diverse segments of the American public to neo-liberal policies. Utilizing the power of the established press, electronic media, and talk radio as sites of cultural politics, conservatives have used their massive financial resources and foundations to influence various segments of the culture industry and national entertainment media.[7] Conservative foundations and groups also have played a pivotal role in educating and persuading a new generation of public intellectuals to wage a relentless battle against all facets of democratic life; groups disadvantaged by race, age, gender, class, and lack of citizenship bear the brunt of this vicious attack. With profound irony, conservative forces have appropriated Antonio Gramsci's celebrated insight that "every relationship of 'hegemony' is necessarily an educational relationship."[8] In doing so, they have reasserted the role of culture as an educational force for social and economic reproduction and have waged an intense ideological battle both within various cultural sites, such as the media, and over important cultural spheres, such as public schools, the arts, and higher education.

The effects of the right's current assault on democracy can be seen in the dismantling of state supports for immigrants, people of color, and working people. As I have pointed out throughout this book, such attacks are evident in the passage of social policies that promote deindustrialization, downsizing, and free market reforms. As an example, recent welfare reform legislation will prohibit over 3.5 million children from receiving any type of government assistance and thus will add more youth to the ranks of over 14.7 million children already living in poverty in the United States.[9] As conservative policies move away from a politics of social investment to one of social containment, state services are hollowed out and reduced to their more repressive functions—discipline, control, and surveillance.[10] This is evident not only in states such as California and Florida, which spend more to incarcerate people than to educate their college-age populations, but also in the disproportionate number of African American males throughout the country who are being imprisoned or placed under the control of the criminal justice system.[11] The results of this battle against democracy and social and economic justice also can be seen in a resurgent racism, marked by anti-immigrant legislation such as Proposition 209 in California, the dismantling of affirmative action, and the reemergence of racist ideologies attempting to prove that differences in intelligence are both racially distinctive and genetically determined.[12] In this instance, racially coded attacks on criminals, the underclass, and welfare mothers are legitimated, in part, through a politically invigorated rhetoric of social Darwinism that both scapegoats people of color while simultaneously blaming them for the social problems that result in their exploitation, suffering, and oppression.[13]

As part of this broader assault on democracy, public education has become one of the most contested public spheres in political life at the turn of the century. More than any other institution, public schools serve as a dangerous reminder of both the promise and the shortcomings of the social, political, and economic forces that shape society. Embodying the contradictions of the larger society, public schools provide a critical referent for measuring the degree to which American society fulfills its obligation to provide all students with the knowledge and skills necessary to participate in and shape democratic public life. As sites that reflect the nation's alleged commitment to the legacy of democracy, schools both challenge and threaten attempts by conservatives and liberals alike to separate "choice" from the discourse of democracy and equity, and to diminish citizenship to a largely privatized affair in which civic responsibilities are reduced to the act of consuming. A euphemism for privatization, "choice" relieves schools of the pretense of serving the public good. Institutions are no longer designed to benefit all members of the community, schools are now refashioned in market terms designed to serve the narrow interests of individual consumers and national economic policies.

Dismissing the role that schools might play as democratic public spheres, conservatives have redefined the meaning and purpose of schooling in accordance with the interests of global capitalism. As financial support for public schools dries up, conservatives increasingly attempt to harness all educational institutions to corporate control through calls for privatization, vouchers, and so-called school choice programs. Rewriting the tradition of schooling as a public good, conservatives draw attention away from equity as an integral part of excellence at the same time as they subsume the political mission of schooling within the ideology and logic of the market. Similarly, conservatives have waged a relentless attack on teacher unions, called for the return of authoritarian teaching approaches, and endorsed learning by drill and rote memorization. In this scenario, public education is replaced by the call for privately funded educational institutions that can safely ignore civil rights, exclude students who are disenfranchised by virtue of class or race, and conveniently blur the lines between religion and the state.

With this attack on education, we are witnessing both the elimination of public school as a potential site for expanding the public good and the realignment of the mission of higher education within the discourse and ideology of the corporate world.[14] Within this perspective, higher education is aggressively shorn of its utopian impulses. Undermined as a repository of critical thinking, writing, teaching, and learning, universities are refashioned to meet the interests of commerce and regulation. In the current onslaught against non-commercial public spheres, the mission of the university becomes instrumental; it is redesigned largely to serve corporate interests whose aim is to restructure higher education along the lines of global capitalism. In specific terms, this means emphasizing instrumental rather than substantive knowledge, shifting power away from faculty to administrations, and corporatizing the culture of the university.[15] As the college curriculum is stripped of those subjects (typically in the humanities) that do not translate immediately into market considerations, programs are downsized and reduced to service programs for business. Not only does instrumental knowledge replace substantive knowledge as the basis for research, writing, and teaching, but university intellectuals are reduced to low-level technocrats. Their role is to manage and legitimate the downsizing, knowledge production, and labor practices that characterize the institutional power and culture of the corporate oriented university.

The defining principle of the current right-wing attack against higher education and public schooling is the dismantling of all public spheres that refuse to be defined strictly by the instrumental logic of the market. Hence the battle waged over education must be understood as part of a much broader struggle for democratic public life, the political function of culture, the role of intellectuals, and the importance of pedagogy as a political and moral practice in shaping various aspects of daily life. At stake here is the issue of how we "think" politics in Gramscian terms, that is, how we create a new culture by reformulating the meaning of cultural politics, intellectual engagement, and educational change.[16] In short, how do we reassert the primacy of a non-dogmatic, progressive politics by analyzing how culture as a force for resistance is related to power, education, and agency? What is needed is an understanding of how culture shapes the everyday lives of people: how culture constitutes a defining principle for understanding how struggles over meaning, identity, social practices, and institutional machineries of power can be waged while inserting the educational back into the political and expanding it by recognizing the "educational force of our whole social and cultural experience [as one] that actively and profoundly teaches."[17]

Gramsci's legacy is important for progressives because he provides a wide-ranging and insightful analysis of how education functions as part of a wider political set of discourses and social relations aimed at promoting ideological and structural change. But in spite of Gramsci's politics and intentions, conservatives have used his work to legitimate a profoundly reactionary view of education and the processes of learning and persuasion. Here I analyze in detail how Gramsci's work has been appropriated by education professor Harold Entwistle in his book *Antonio Gramsci: Conservative Schooling for Radical Politics* and more recently by E. D. Hirsch in his book *The Schools We Need* to push a deeply conservative educational agenda. Gramsci's writings on education do represent a problematic legacy for progressives. However, I argue that when read within the appropriate historical context and in relation to his revolutionary project, Gramsci's work enables radical educators to rethink the political nature of educational work as part of a broader struggle for developing the relationship between learning and democratic social change on one hand and committed intellectual practice and political struggle on the other.[18]

APPROPRIATING GRAMSCI

Although the work of Harold Entwistle and E. D. Hirsch is separated by a decade, both men share similar views about the value of a conservative approach to schooling.[19] Not only do both authors legitimate schools as agents of social and economic reproduction, they advocate classroom practices based on learning a common culture, rigid disciplinary rules, an authoritarian educational model, and a standardized curricula. At the same time, it is important to note that Entwistle considers Gramsci's work far more seriously and makes some valuable contributions both in his critiques of some progressive forms of political education and in his suggestions for rethinking the politics of adult education. In his work on Gramsci, Hirsch attempts to reappropriate Entwistle in the service of a right-wing conservatism that blames educational progressives in the United States for the decline of teaching and learning in the public schools. Hirsch's "discovery" that Gramsci is actually a poster boy for conservative thought combines the bad faith of misrepresentation with the reductionism of an ideological fervor that seems to make a mockery of political sense and historical accuracy.[20] While the reasons for the appropriation of Gramsci's work by a diverse body of radical educators may be open to interpretation, it certainly stretches the bounds of plausibility when Hirsch aligns Gramsci with contemporary, right-wing educational theorists such as Diane Ravitch and Charles Sykes. Not only does such an appropriation represent a form of theoretical disingenuousness and political opportunism, it is also an affront to everything that Gramsci stood for as a renegade Marxist revolutionary.

Entwistle and Hirsch share a view of schooling that stands in sharp contrast to the radical educational theories of their time; yet they appropriate from Gramsci's work a rationale for conservative teaching practices as part of their attempt to redefine the relationship between schooling and society on one hand and intellectuals and their social responsibilities on the other. Although Entwistle's book provides a more extensive reading of Gramsci, Hirsch applies the implications of such a conservative interpretation directly to matters affecting teaching and learning in the United States. Moreover, Hirsch draws upon the work of Gramsci and that of his own conservative contemporaries in a spurious effort to produce what he calls a "pragmatic" and bipartisan, rather than "ideological" and conservative, agenda for educational reform. In what follows, I consider how both authors appropriate Gramsci and analyze the implications of their work for a theory of schooling and education.

Harold Entwistle's book represents one of the first comprehensive analyses of the relevance of Gramsci's writings on schooling for educational theory and practice.[21] Providing his own detailed interpretation of those writings, Entwistle rejects as misguided the way Gramsci's work was interpreted previously and excoriates "new sociologists of education" as well as other radical educational theorists who rose to prominence in England in the 1970s and 1980s. After resurrecting the "real" Gramsci, Entwistle proceeds to dismiss those radical critics who have allegedly misinterpreted Gramsci's work. The remainder of Entwistle's book focuses on the relevance of Gramsci's writings for adult education; it ends with the "remarkable" conclusion that the lesson to be learned from Gramsci's work is that schools do not provide the setting for "a radical, counterhegemonic education."[22]

To Entwistle, Gramsci is a "stern" taskmaster whose views on discipline, knowledge, and hegemony render him more compatible with Karl Popper and Jacques Barzun (both of whom are referred to positively) than the likes of Karl Marx, Paulo Freire, or, for that matter, even John Dewey. If we are to take Entwistle's version of Gramsci seriously as a model for socialist education, then we will have to accept the claim that Gramsci wholeheartedly supported a deference to authority, the rote memorizing of facts, and a subservience to imposed standards as core educational principles. Such a claim is hardly consistent with Gramsci's call for an educational practice and project aimed at generating "more and more organic intellectuals from the children of the peasantry and the proletariat."[23]

Conservative literary theorist E. D. Hirsch echoes a similar argument. He describes Gramsci's work as a critical response to Giovanni Gentile's educational reforms, enacted under Benito Mussolini in the 1920s—reforms that emphasized "emotion," "feeling," and the "most immediate needs of the child." The failure of these reforms, according to Hirsch, served as proof of the inadequacy of what he incorrectly terms the central tenets of critical educational theory. In opposition to this form of "progressive" pedagogy, Hirsch argues that Gramsci offers a rationale for conservative methods such as "phonics and memorization of the multiplication table," claiming that they are necessary for "the oppressed classes to learn how to read, write, and communicate—and to gain enough traditional knowledge to understand the worlds of nature and culture surrounding them."[24]

What Hirsch and Entwistle fail to acknowledge in their selective readings of Gramsci is that his concern with "facts" and intellectual rigor makes sense only as a critique of inane methodologies that separate facts from values, learning from understanding, and emotion from the intellect. As social theorist David Forgacs points out in the introduction to *An Antonio Gramsci Reader*, Gramsci

> begins not from the point of view of the teacher but from that of the learner, and he emphasizes that the learning process is a movement toward self-knowledge, self-mastery and thus liberation. Education is not a matter of handing out "encyclopedic knowledge" but of developing and disciplining the awareness which the learner already possesses.[25]

Gramsci's emphasis on intellectual rigor and discipline can be understood only as part of a broader concern for students to develop a critical understanding of how the past informs the present so that they can liberate themselves from the ideologies and commonsense assumptions that form the core beliefs of the dominant order. Gramsci was quite clear on the distinction between learning facts that enlarged one's perception of the larger social order and simply gathering information. Even in his earlier writings, before Gramsci was imprisoned, he understood the relationship between an educational practice of rote memorization and the conservative nature of the culture it served to legitimate. For instance, he wrote in 1916:

We must break the habit of thinking that culture is encyclopedic knowledge whereby man [sic] is viewed as a mere container in which to pour and conserve empirical data or brute disconnected facts which he will have to subsequently pigeonhole in his brain as in the columns of a dictionary so as to be able to eventually respond to the varied stimuli of the external world. This form of culture is truly harmful, especially to the proletariat. It only serves to create misfits, people who believe themselves superior to the rest of humanity because they have accumulated in their memory a certain quantity of facts and dates which they cough up at every opportunity to almost raise a barrier between themselves and others.[26]

Hirsch ignores Gramsci's critique of encyclopedic knowledge, arguing that

romantic anti-intellectualism and developmentalism [critical thinking and critical social theory], as Gramsci understood, are luxuries of the merchant class that the poor cannot afford. . . . Today, the Enlightenment view of the value of knowledge is the only view we can afford. When the eighteenth-century Encyclopedists attempted to systematize human knowledge in a set of books, they were placing their hope for progress in the evergrowing experience of human kind."[27]

For Hirsch, the production of knowledge by the middleclass is brought about with only good intentions. Hirsch seems unable to critically engage the relationship between knowledge and power or that which exists between ideology and politics. To address how culture and power combine to produce knowledge that often legitimates particular racial, class, and gendered interests would work against his general educational program: to teach children a core knowledge base of "facts." For Hirsch the most important use of encyclopedic knowledge is in inculcating mental discipline;

moreover, the primary purpose of education is not only to transmit such knowledge but to prevent it from being undermined by forms of "anti-intellectualism" in the American educational community whose legacy Hirsch argues extends from "'home economics' and 'shop' in the 1920s to all forms of 'critical thinking and problem solving skills' in the 1990s."[28]

For Gramsci, the production of knowledge and its reception and transformation was historical, dialectical, and critical. He rejected mere factuality and demanded that schooling be "formative, while being 'instructive.'" The educational task entailed, in part, "mitigating and rendering more fertile the dogmatic approach which must inevitably characterize these first few years."[29] Such a task was not easy and demanded, on one hand, the necessity "to place limits on libertarian ideologies"; on the other hand, it was necessary to recognize that "the elements of struggle against the mechanical and Jesuitical school have become unhealthily exaggerated."[30] Underlying Gramsci's educational system is a principle in which a comfortable humanism is replaced by a hard-headed radicalism, not a radicalism that falsely separates necessity and spontaneity, discipline and the acquisition of basic skills from imagination, but rather one that integrates them.

In contrast, Entwistle and Hirsch interpret Gramsci's view of schooling as one that surrenders teaching to dull routine. In doing so they imply that such an educational practice can be and should be maintained at the expense of the spirit. The interconnections between discipline and critical thinking in Gramsci's view of schooling lend support to a conservative notion of education only if the concept of physical discipline and self-control is abstracted from his emphasis on the importance of developing a militant political project, one "which demands the formation of a militant, self-conscious proletariat that will fight unyieldingly for its right to govern itself. . . ."[31] In other words, Gramsci's claim that, for the student, "it will always be an effort to learn physical self-discipline and self-control, the pupil, has, in effect, to undergo psyche-physical training"[32] gets seriously distorted unless understood within the context of his other remarks on learning and intellectual development. Gramsci stressed this view not only in his early writing in 1916 but just as forcefully in the *Notebooks* of 1921-1935. In the latter he writes "Many people have to be persuaded that studying too is a job, and a very tiring one with its own particular apprenticeship involving muscles and nerves as well as *intellect*"[33] (my emphasis).

For Gramsci, there was a dynamic tension between self-discipline and critical understanding. Consequently, what in fact often appears to be a paradox in his work on education is in reality a nuanced and dialectical endorsement of a critical and disciplined educational practice informed by a notion of radical classroom authority. Distinguishing between classroom authority that works in the service of critical agency and authority used to promote conformity and allegiance to the state, Gramsci provides a political referent for criticizing schools that he claims are merely bourgeois affairs. According to Gramsci, any teaching practice has to be examined and implemented within a broader understanding of what the purpose of schooling might become and how such a view of political education articulates with a wider democratic project. Schools, in this instance, are seen as central and formative sites for the production of political identities, for the nurturing of individual struggles to reclaim culture, and for the educating of organic intellectuals. In "Questions of Culture," Gramsci argues that acquiring political power must be matched with the "problem of winning intellectual power."[34] If the school is to offer students of the working class and other subordinate groups the knowledge and skills necessary for political leadership, they cannot be simply, as Hirsch, in particular, would have it, boot camps for the intellectually malleable. Gramsci is quite clear on this issue:

> A school which does not mortgage the child's future, a school that does not force the child's will, his intelligence and growing awareness to run along the tracks to a predetermined station. A

school of freedom and free initiative, not a school of slavery and mechanical precision. The children of proletarians too should have all possibilities open to them; they should be able to develop their own individuality in the optimal way, and hence in the most productive way for both themselves and society.[35]

For Gramsci, any analysis of education can be understood only in relation to existing social and cultural formations and the power relations these imply. Gramsci emphasized that schooling constitutes only one form of political education within a broader network of experience, history, and collective struggle. Given his view of political education, it is difficult to reduce Gramsci's theory of teaching and learning to a rigid methodology such as rote learning, that conservatives endorse without questioning whether it is either implicated in or offers resistance to the mechanisms of consent, common sense, and dominant social relations.

Hirsch enlists Gramsci to justify authoritarian classroom relations in which students are deprived of the basic right to ask questions, address disturbing, urgent issues. This authoritarianism fosters a sense that the learner's point of view is irrelevant. For both Hirsch and many other conservative educators, schools are dysfunctional not because they oppress students from subordinate groups but because the legacy of progressive education emphasizes "'project oriented,' 'hands-on,' 'critical-thinking' and so-called 'democratic education'" rather then a core curriculum of facts and information.[36] Hirsch, in particular, endorses a reductive view of information accumulation in which the critical relationship between culture and power remains largely unexamined, except as a pretext to urge working-class and subordinate groups to master the dominant culture as a way of reproducing the social order. Hirsch makes this point quite clearly:

The oppressed class should be taught to master the tools of power and authority—the ability to read, write, and communicate—and to gain enough traditional knowledge to understand the worlds of nature and culture surrounding them. Children, particularly the children of the poor, should not be encouraged to flourish "naturally," which would keep them ignorant and make them slaves of emotion. They should learn the value of hard work, gain the knowledge that leads to understanding, and master the traditional culture in order to command its rhetoric, as Gramsci himself had learned to do.[37]

The implication here is that any attempt to teaching working-class children the specifics of their histories, experiences, and cultural memories would simply result in a form of educational infantilism. More important, Hirsch misses a central concern that runs throughout Gramsci's work—skills are not universal, and must be addressed within a context that poses particular problems and questions that educators, not to mention students, must grasp and engage. Skills become relevant to the degree that they relate to the historical and social contexts that give them meaning. Similarly, Hirsch assumes that the poor performance of working-class students results from intellectual laziness and has nothing to do with underfunded schools, a diminished tax base, or urban politics. On the contrary, for Hirsch, overcrowded classrooms, inadequate classroom resources, and broken-down school buildings play no role in whether working-class kids and other subordinate groups do well in schools. The real enemy of student learning, according to Hirsch, is the critical legacy of progressivism and its failure to endorse rote learning, a core curriculum, and uniform teaching rather than the force of racial and class bias, poor working conditions for teachers, or poverty.[38]

Of course, while Gramsci was deeply concerned with students learning "facts" and specific forms of knowledge, he did not advocate that the context of such learning was irrelevant. He believed that learning had to be rigorous but meaningful, subject-based but related to practical activities. Appropriating Marx's

"Theses on Feuerbach" (the educator must be educated), Gramsci believed that "the relationship between teacher and pupil is active and reciprocal so that every teacher is always a pupil and every pupil a teacher."[39] By arguing that the teacher-student relationship leaves no room for elitism or sterile pedantry, Gramsci introduces an important principle into the structuring of classroom social relations. The concept of the teacher as a learner suggests that teachers must help students critically appropriate their own histories but also must look critically at their own role as oppositional public intellectuals located within specific cultural formations and relations of power. In this instance, Gramsci not only argues implicitly against forms of authoritarian teaching, he sharply criticizes the assumption that knowledge should be treated unproblematically— beyond the dynamics of interrogation, criticism, and political engagement. Gramsci had no interest in allowing schools to produce a culture that served repressive authority and state power, nor did he have any interest in supporting teachers and intellectuals who were reduced to what he called "experts in legitimation."[40]

Both Hirsch and Entwistle ignore how selective meanings and values are both produced in schools and reinforced by the mechanisms of economic and political control that are active in the dominant society. Hence, Entwistle and Hirsch depoliticize the relationship between power and culture, but Hirsch is especially vehement in legitimating the dominant and oppressive role that schools play in defining what is legitimate knowledge and social practice. For Hirsch, this position translates into a call for a common national curriculum that emphasizes the acquisition of core knowledge and standardized testing.[41] Hirsch has no conception that such a position is at odds with the oppositional project posed by Gramsci—education as a means to create organic intellectuals whose task is to identify the social interests behind power; challenge traditional understandings of culture, power, and politics; and share such knowledge as the basis for organizing diverse forms of class struggle in order to create a socialist society. Class struggle or the goal of socialism could not be further removed from Hirsch's politics.

Rather than acknowledge the need to place value on the "disrespected identities and the cultural products of maligned groups,"[42] Hirsch wants to "save" underprivileged kids by stripping them of their identities and histories while assimilating them into the dominant culture. Curriculum in these terms provides the legitimization for forms of middle-class cultural capital that serve as an institutionally sanctioned bunker against learning and living with differences.[43] Hirsch argues that while teaching multicultur-alism may have some value, it ultimately is disruptive to lower-class students because it is approached through "amateur psychological" efforts [that] fail because [they result] in lies to children about their achievements . . . and lead to further erosion of their self esteem."[44] It does not occur to Hirsch that schools may be inadvertently spawning failing students through racially motivated models of teaching, tracking, and evaluation. Should we assume that the curricula that represent middle-class cultural capital, the ultimate referent against which the narratives of history, identity, and social experience should always be judged, is undoubtedly uplifting for working-class kids? Or that the warehousing and tracking often built in to school curricula to the disadvantage of racial, class, and gender minorities work to their advantage? This position is not merely naive, it is a construct of reactionary politics parading as common sense and is completely at odds with Gramsci's view of the role that education should play in liberating subordinate groups.

Unlike Gramsci, neither Entwistle nor Hirsch provides a critical language to deconstruct the basis of privileges that are accorded the dominant culture. They make no attempt to consider culture as the shared and lived principles of life, characteristic of different groups and classes as these emerge within unequal relations of power and struggle. Nor do Entwistle and Hirsch critically engage how questions of power; history; and race, gender, and class privilege work to codify specific ideological educational practices as merely the accumulation of disinterested knowledge "that can be exchanged on the world market for upward mobility."[45] In effect, they de-emphasize unequally valued cultural styles and the ways in which dominant educational practices work to disparage the multiple languages, histories, and experiences at work in a multicultural society.

Hirsch, in particular, ends up legitimating a homogenizing cultural discourse that institutionalizes various policing techniques to safeguard the interests and power of dominant groups. In the end, both Entwistle and Hirsch support a view of culture and knowledge as monolithic: the product of a single, durable history and vision at odds with the notion and politics of difference. The cultural politics at work in this view of education is silent regarding the validity and importance of the experiences of women, blacks, and other groups excluded from the narrative of mainstream history and culture. Thus there emerges no critical understanding of Gramsci's focus on culture as a field of struggle or as a space of competing interests in which dominant and subordinate groups make sense of their circumstances and lives within unequal hierarchies of power and possibility.

Entwistle and Hirsch do more than offer an unenlightened and reductive reading of culture; they appropriate the Gramscian position that schools are agencies of social and cultural reproduction and in doing so defend this position rather than criticize it. Rather than understanding culture as a storehouse of immutable facts, behaviors, and practices, Gramsci relates culture inextricably to the outcomes of struggle over the complex and often contradictory processes of learning, persuasion, agency, and leadership. Culture is about the production and authorization of particular ways of life transmitted in schools through the overt and hidden curricula so as to legitimate the cultural capital of dominant groups while marginalizing the voices of subordinate ones. If power is related to culture in the discourses of Entwistle and Hirsch, the theoretical consequence is a notion of culture cleansed of its own complicity in furthering social relations and educational practices that reproduce the worst dimensions of schooling. For example, missing from this analysis is any understanding of the increasing corporate takeover of some schools and its effects on teachers and students; also absent is any consideration of how poverty, racism, and gender bias structure the school curricula, affect the distribution of financial resources among schools, and shape the organization of the teaching labor force. While Hirsch's reading of Gramsci is crude compared to Entwistle's extensive analysis, both theorists share a conservative ideological project in their reading of the role of intellectuals and the purpose of schooling. Both men represent different versions of the same ideology, one that is deeply committed to expunging democracy of its critical and emancipatory possibilities. In what follows, I conclude by pointing to aspects of Gramsci's work that might be useful for developing some important theoretical principles for a critical theory of schooling and education.

THINKING LIKE GRAMSCI: RECLAIMING THE STRUGGLE OVER SCHOOLING

Given the current assault on schooling and public life in general, it is imperative that progressive educators develop a language of critique and possibility—a language that is both critical and offers productive alternatives—along with new strategies for understanding and intervention to reclaim and reinvigorate the struggle to sustain public schooling as a central feature of democratic life. Gramsci's work is enormously helpful in this regard because it forcefully reminds us that any attempt to address the nature and purpose of schooling must be part of a broader comprehensive politics of social change. Schooling, in Gramsci's terms, was always part of some larger ensemble "of relationships headed and moved by authority and power."[46] Hence the struggle over schooling is inextricably linked to the struggle against abusive state power on one hand and the battle for "creating more equitable and just public spheres within and outside of educational institutions"[47] on the other. Gramsci also makes clear that both teaching and educational policy are the outcome of struggles over both the relations of meaning and institutional relations of power and that such struggles cannot be abstracted from the construction of national identity and what it means to be an active citizen. In this context, educational practice is inextricably grounded in a normative position and project aimed at overcoming the stark inequalities and forms of oppression suffered by subordinate groups. The theoretical and ideological contours of Gramsci's project offer no immediate solutions to problems faced by American educators. Nor can Gramsci's work simply be appropriated outside of his own history and the challenges it posed. What his vast writings do provide are opportunities for raising questions about what it means to rethink the struggle over schooling in our own time, a time that demands theoretical rigor, moral courage, and political boldness. Gramsci's analysis of the political and social role of culture in establishing and reproducing the power of the modern state represents a crucial theoretical sphere for progressive educators. Central to his analysis is not only the important recognition of culture as a terrain of consent and struggle but also the political imperative to analyze how diverse groups make meaning of their lives. For Gramsci, the politics of culture was inseparable from a politics that provided the conditions for educators to think critically about how knowledge is produced, taken up, and transformed as a force for social change and collective struggle.

The practical relevance of his work on culture and teaching can be made clearer by commenting further on two issues: the role of basic education and the relevance of Gramsci's call for teaching practices that instill in young children an appreciation for self-discipline and an array of intellectual skills. While it is crucial to recognize Gramsci's call for treating various levels of schooling as sites of struggle, it is equally imperative to recognize that education for him was fundamental to furnishing young people and adults with the knowledge and skills that would enable them to be able to govern and not just be governed. Moreover, and equally important, citizens should be able use civil society as a public enclave from which to organize their moral and political energies as acts of affirmation, resistance, and struggle.

While Gramsci did not believe that state-sponsored schools alone would provide the conditions for social change, he did suggest they had a role to play in nourishing the tension between the democratic principles of civil society and the dominating principles of capitalism and corporate power. The project of liberal education for Gramsci was wedded to the fundamental socialist principle of educating the complete person—one who could comment broadly on politics, culture, and society—rather than the traditional concern with educating the masses as specialists, technocrats, and other professional experts. Gramsci insisted that critical intellectuals had to use their education in order to both know more than their enemies and to make such knowledge consequential by bringing it to bear in all those sites of everyday life where the struggle for and against the powerful was being waged. While Gramsci's work is neither transparent nor merely transportable to different historical and political contexts, it seems reasonable to argue that education for him was deeply involved in the project of furthering economic and political democracy, and that such a project is especially important today for articulating a progressive, if not radical, defense of public and higher education. In the broadest sense, Gramsci's position would offer progressives a theoretical rationale for challenging the existing efforts of corporate culture to define public and higher education as a private rather than public good. Such an education also would serve to challenge the dominant society's increasing pressure to use the liberal arts to assert the primacy of consumer rights over citizen rights, commercial values over democratic values.

Gramsci's emphasis on the importance of culture and teaching in constructing a social subject rather than an adaptive, depoliticized consuming subject provided the context for his insistence on the importance of skills, rigor, discipline, and hard work. For instance, his often-cited call for teaching young children skills cannot be considered, as I previously argued, as simply legitimating a conservative educational theory. Gramsci recognized that, within the "new" Italian reforms, which argued that people should simply discover truths for themselves, children were being deprived of basic skills that would enable them to read, write, and struggle over complex problems as well as prepare them to use such skills to expand their capacities as critical intellectuals and citizens. For Gramsci, educational approaches that refused to deal with such issues reneged on using their authority to provide the skills, knowledge, and discipline necessary for young children to assume the role of critical or organic intellectuals. Gramsci rightly challenged those educational practices that affirmed the alleged natural development of the child as a rationale for devaluing classroom authority. Authority in this scenario did not pass from teacher to student, it was simply made invisible. In short, such practices provided a rationale for Mussolini's educational clerks to conceal their authority while limiting students', especially working-class students', abilities to learn the skills necessary for understanding, critical engagement, resistance, and more important, civic struggle. Hirsch misses the point: Gramsci's analysis is not a justification of rote learning but an attempt to analyze the context for teaching young children the skills they will need to be engaged citizens and to call into question any educational practice that refuses to name the political interests that shape its own project.

For Gramsci, the learning of skills, discipline, and rigor was not valuable in and of itself. These subjects were meaningful only when seen as part of a broader radical project, one that embraced authority in the service of social change and understood culture as the terrain in which such authority became both the object of autocritique and the basis for social analysis and struggle. Hence Gramsci's emphasis on culture as a medium of politics and power is important for progressive educators because it challenges theories of social and cultural reproduction that overemphasize power as a force of domination. Gramsci is extremely sensitive to the productive nature of power as a complex and often contradictory site of domination, struggle, and resistance. Long before French philosopher Michel Foucault, Gramsci questioned how culture is deployed, represented, and taken up in order to understand how power works to produce not merely forms of domination but also complicity and dissent. Gramsci's thorough analysis of culture and power provides an important theoretical model for linking cultural politics and the discourse of critique to a language of hope, struggle, and possibility. Of course, Gramsci does not provide, nor should we expect him to offer, a blueprint for such a struggle, but his view of leadership and his theory of intellectuals offer a powerful challenge to those conservative ideologues and theoreticians who reduce the function of intellectuals either to their technical expertise or pay unquestioned homage to them as the cultural guardians and servants of oppressive state power.

Gramsci's theory of hegemony as a form of social leadership and cultural teaching is also invaluable as an element of critical educational thought. By emphasizing the educational force of culture, Gramsci expands the sphere of the political by pointing to those diverse spaces in which cultural practices are deployed, lived, and mobilized in the service of knowledge, power, and authority. For Gramsci, learning and politics were inextricably related and took place not merely in schools but in a vast array of public sites. While he could not anticipate how knowledge and power would be configured within the postmodern technologies that emerged in the age of the high-speed computer and other electronic media, Gramsci did recognize the political and educational significance of popular culture and the need to take it seriously when mapping the relations between everyday life and the formations of power. Clearly, Gramsci's recognition that the study of everyday life and popular culture needed to be incorporated into a struggle for power and leadership is as relevant today as it was in his own time. This is especially true when challenging or attempting to transform the modernist curriculum that is steeped in its celebration of the traditional Western canon and its refusal to address the histories, experiences, and cultures of marginalized groups.

If critical educators are to make a case for the context-specific nature of teaching—a teaching that not only negotiates difference but takes seriously the imperative to make knowledge meaningful so that it might become critical and transformative—they must expand curricula to include those elements of popular culture that play a powerful role in shaping the desires, needs, and identities of students. This is not to suggest that students ignore the Western-oriented curriculum or dispense with print culture as much as redefine the relationship between knowledge and power and how the latter is used to mobilize desire, shape identities, and secure particular forms of authority. It is not enough for students simply to be literate in the print culture of the humanities or in the histories of oppressed groups. Critical education demands that teachers and students also must learn how to read critically the new technological and visual cultures that exercise a powerful influence over their lives as well as their conception of what it means to be a social subject engaged in acts of responsible citizenship. In addition, they must master the tools of these technologies, whether they are computer programming, video production, or magazine production, in order to create alternative public spheres that are actively engaged in shaping what Gramsci referred to as a new and oppositional culture.

The questions that Gramsci raises about education, culture, and political struggle also have important ramifications for theorizing about educators as public intellectuals and how they might challenge the institutional and cultural terrains through which dominant authority is secured and state power is legitimated. Film theorist Marcia Landy is on target in arguing that one of Gramsci's most important contributions to political change is the recognition that the "study of intellectuals and their production is synonymous with the study of political power."[48] Gramsci's concern with the formation and responsibility of intellectuals stems from his recognition that they are central not only to fostering critical consciousness, demystifying dominant social relations, and disrupting common sense but that they also had a responsibility to locate political education in the context of a more comprehensive project. This project was to be aimed at the liberation of oppressed peoples as historical agents within the framework of a revolutionary culture.

According to Gramsci, political education demanded that intellectuals could not be neutral; nor could they ignore the most pressing social and political problems of their times. Within a Gramscian framework, the new intellectuals had little to do with the traditional humanist project of speaking for a universal culture or abstracting culture from the workings of power, history, and struggle in the name of an arid professionalism. As cultural critics, Gramscian intellectuals refused to define culture merely as a refined aesthetic of taste and civility. On the contrary, their task was to provide modes of leadership that bridged the gap between criticism and politics, theory and action, and traditional educational institutions and everyday life. For Gramsci, the role of the engaged intellectual was a matter of moral compassion and practical politics aimed at addressing the gap between theory and practice.

Gramsci's analysis suggests that contemporary intellectuals take up the public tasks of becoming what he calls "permanent persuaders and not just orators."[49] Such persuasion takes place not merely in the isolated, safe confines of the universities but in those spheres of daily life in which subordinated groups bear the weight of coercion and domination. Clearly, Gramsci's discourse on the education and political function of "organic" intellectuals provides an important theoretical background for questioning the meaning and function of public and higher education at a time when they are not only selling their curricula, space, and buildings to corporations but undermining even the humanist understanding of the intellectual as a purveyor of art and culture. Moreover, Gramsci's view of the political educator provides an important corrective to the conservative notion that intellectuals should be scorned as radicals because they "take sides" or reject the view that the highest value of scholarly activity is disinterested, dispassionate inquiry. Gramsci recognized that there was nothing either apolitical or value free to be found in the conservative call for an ideology-free education. In contemporary terms, such an education is increasingly being offered under the auspices of conservative institutions such as the Olin Foundation, which are more than willing to finance curricula reform, endowed chairs, and grant money to promote "value-free" free enterprise reforms.

Gramsci's work does more than challenge the reduction of intellectuals to corporate boosters; it also broadens the meaning and role of intellectuals in terms of their social functions and individual capabilities. Changes in the mass media, modes of production, and socioeconomic needs of the state enlarge the role that intellectuals play in exercising authority, producing knowledge, and securing consent. For Gramsci, intellectuals played a crucial political and educational role in integrating thought and action for subordinate groups. This role was part of a broader project to assert the primacy of political education far beyond the limited circle of party hacks or university academics. Moreover, Gramsci is not just suggesting that marginal groups generate their own intellectuals; he is also broadening the conditions for the production of knowledge and the range of sites through which learning for self-determination can occur. This is an important issue because it legitimates the call for progressives to create their own intellectuals and public spheres both within and outside of traditional sites of learning as part of a broader effort to expand the sources of resistance and the dynamics of democratic struggle.

Finally, Gramsci's radical theory of political education provides an ethical language for grounding intellectual work in a project that not only demands commitment and risk but also recognizes the ethical imperative to bear witness to collective suffering and to provide a referent for translating such a recognition into social engagement. This project suggests that intellectuals must be self-critical in order to address the nature of their own institutional locations, self-interests, and privileges. Moreover, they must be in constant dialogue with cultural workers who deploy their authority as teachers, researchers, theorists, and planners in order to expose and transform the oppressive conditions through which individuals and groups are constructed and differentiated. For Gramsci, critical intellectuals must begin by acknowledging their engagement with the "density, complexity, and historical-semantic value of culture," an engagement that grounds them in the power-making possibilities of politics.[50] Currently Gramsci's work serves as a reminder that "democracy requires a certain kind of citizen . . . citizens who feel responsible for something more than their own well-feathered little corner; citizens who want to participate in society's affairs, who insist on it; citizens with backbones; citizens who hold their ideas about democracy at the deepest level."[51] Education in this context becomes central to principled leadership, critical agency, and the ongoing task of keeping the idea of justice alive while struggling collectively on many fronts to restructure society in the interest of expanding the possibilities of democracy. Gramsci's reading of culture, political education, the role and responsibility of intellectuals, and the necessity to struggle in the interests of equality and justice are crucial starting points for progressives to rethink and address the current assault on public schooling and the basic foundations of democracy itself.

FIVE

Paulo Freire, Prophetic Thought, and the Politics of Hope

> To think of history as possibility is to recognize educa-
> tion as possibility. It is to recognize that if education
> cannot do everything, it can achieve some things. . . .
> One of our challenges as educators is to discover what
> historically is possible in the sense of contributing
> toward the transformation of the world, giving rise to a
> world that is rounder, less angular, more humane.
> —Paulo Freire, "A Dialogue: Culture, Language, and Race"

ERASING HOPE

Fueled by the initial success of their attack on the welfare state in
the early 1980s, many conservatives and liberals joined forces in
dismantling all public spheres not governed by the imperatives of
the market.[1] In addition, they have conducted an ongoing and
relentless attack on public spaces that provide intellectuals with the
opportunity to "openly debate issues of vital public concern,
publish tracts and newspapers, engage in heated, but civic-spirited

discussions"[2] and deploy political practices that help keep alive, as the poet Robert Haas puts it, "the idea of justice, which is going dead in us all the time."[3] But the threat to critical intellectual work is evident not only in attempts to eliminate oppositional public spheres that connect educators, artists, and others to an insurgent cultural politics.[4] The very notion of culture as a terrain of struggle—that is, the recognition of culture and power as a constitutive political and educational practice—is, as I have mentioned previously, also under attack by a growing number of left-oriented progressives. Mired in a deep-rooted cynicism, many left intellectuals discount the very concept of the political. In some cases, self-serving discourses about the "reactionary" nature of hope are used to buttress the dismissal of any form of cultural politics that makes a call for social change. Dismissing such calls as morally dogmatic, proponents of this position suggest that any political project is by default totalitarian and oppressive; these advocates conveniently leave it to others to judge the basis of their own claims. This type of critical engagement has no overriding object, goal, or purpose, except to suggest that all projects of emancipation are hopelessly essentialist and dogmatic. It is almost impossible to find in this work any notion of what constitutes an act of resistance or what such an act would be expected to achieve as a form of practical politics.[5] Unfortunately, such work can account neither for spaces of contestation nor for justifying the intimate link between theory and action.

A second form of critique that legitimates political indifference and has gained ascendancy in academic circles derives from a version of poststructuralist theory—a radical critique of conventional views of culture, language, and reason—that emphasizes the primacy of dialogue and discursive formations and celebrates notions of indeterminacy, performance, and transgression. In these approaches, cultural politics focuses largely on events as cultural texts and how they are "presented, 'licensed,' or made 'excessive.'"[6] Within this dialogue, there is a growing tendency, especially as the idea becomes more popular in North America, of "privileging cultural texts over practice as the site of the social and political."[7] Texts, in this approach, do not privilege critical analysis but performance, and engaging texts becomes an occasion for a kind of linguistic display. The exclusive emphasis on texts, however, runs the risk of reproducing processes of reification and isolation, as when the performative is framed outside of the context of history, power, and politics. In this instance, texts become trapped within a formalism that often succumbs to viewing issues such as one's commitment to the "Other," the ethical duty to decide between what is better and what is worse, and, by extension, human rights as meaningless, irrelevant, or leftovers of a bygone age. In its most reductive moment, this approach to cultural politics falls prey to a one-sided focus on politics as rhetoric in which the political dimension of such practice "is rendered invisible by virtue of being regarded as purely performative. . . . What one performs is rendered immaterial. Whatever 'is' is simply a performance."[8] Missing from these approaches is any attempt to specify the "larger political effects of struggles over meaning and identity in the public sphere."[9] Moreover, such approaches fail to link questions of representation to issues of power, economics, and politics. Consequently they have little to say about the effects of such discourses in the larger society or the material conditions of their production (critical theorist Herbert Marcuse insightfully referred to this type of work as "scholarshit."[10]). Moreover, this type of discourse is lifeless and lacks any "sense of the texture of social oppression and the harm that it does."[11] Whatever claim to the performative and transgressive it makes, it is purely gestural and empty—a boldness that threatens no one and offers only the false hope of irony and playfulness without the burden of practical engagements, commitments, and social action.[12]

Such attacks on the related notion of hope, politics, and social change are not without some value in that they point to the necessity to revive the great Brazilian educator Paulo Freire's notion of "concrete" utopianism, which embraces a notion of social change that is historical, conditional, and contextual. For Freire, utopianism consists of the seemingly outmoded idea that education, in the broad sense, consists of intervening in the world in order to change it. Freire believed that intervention could not be simply reduced to a discursive act; nor could it succumb to the seductions of contemporary political and epistemological relativism. Informed by the practicality of a hope that was anticipatory and not simply compensatory or messianic (the promise of a perfect future), intervention in Freire's political landscape assumes the responsibility of challenging and transforming oppressive social relations rooted in language, everyday life, and material formations of power. In Freire's terms, a utopian-based act of intervention means struggling for "radical changes in society in such areas as economics, human relations, property, the right to employment, to land, to education, and to health."[13]

Freire's work is especially important in providing a critical analysis of the relationship between the political and the educational. It provides a redefinition of educators, students, and other progressives as border crossers and public intellectuals who engage in intertextual negotiations across different sites of cultural production. The concepts of border crossing and public intellectual emphasize both the shifting nature of oppositional-public spheres and the problems they pose as locations of identity formation, politics, and struggle; they also draw attention to the kinds of cultural work that increasingly takes place in the border space between "high" and popular culture; between the institution and the street; between the public and the private. Intellectual work in this instance is marked by forms of invention, specificity, and critique as well as an ongoing recognition of the need to inquire into the conditions necessary for people to become agents capable of shaping the crucial conditions and forces that impact on their lives.

One of Freire's lasting contributions to radical change has been his analysis of radical education and his emphasis on viewing educational work as rooted in the specifics of particular struggles and contexts. Freire never saw his own work as simply a methodology; he believed it was a way to understand how educational practices are deployed within discursive formations and material relations of power and as a way to see how the practices themselves shape the conditions for challenging and altering such power in the interest of a transformative, democratic politics.

Because I believe that theoretical work at its best should be used to respond to particular contexts and struggles, I first sketch the current crisis facing public education in the United States. My argument here builds on chapters 3 and 4 and supports the notion that as public education becomes corporatized, it defaults on its promise to provide young people with the skills and knowledge they need to actively participate in shaping history and the existing social order.

Second, I turn to Freire's work to provide a theoretical basis for rethinking the nature of the crisis of schooling and public life. Also, I refer to Freire's work as a way to affirm the political, cultural, and social as central categories through which to redefine the crucial connection between educational theory and practice on one hand and cultural politics and social change on the other. Paulo Freire's work is important because it rigorously challenges the cynicism and hopelessness that permeates much of the debate about American schooling. As one of the most important radical educators of the twentieth century, Freire provides an exemplary model of what it means to be an oppositional public intellectual rather than a public relations intellectual. Not only does his work cross the normally segregated zones of the academy and the larger world of politics and social engagement, it brings together the unexpected maps and possibilities of theory with the practical politics of educational considerations as they intersect with everyday life and broader social formations.

At the same time, I want to make it clear that although I make a claim for the importance of Freire's work as one that challenges a "hope that has lost its bearings,"[14] I do not believe that his educational theories and experiences can simply be transported from their original Latin American context and applied in grid-like fashion to the United States. Freire insisted on many occasions that his work was not subject to narrow tactical or methodological applications.[15] But his educational philosophy along with its revolutionary politics, theory of practice, and strong commitment to the everyday culture of the oppressed does provide educators with a sense of solidarity, courage, and helpful guidance. Similarly, if educators are to be faithful to the spirit of Freire's work, they must treat it with critical respect rather than reverence. In other words, his work must be subject to continuing debate regarding its political and educational relevance and theoretically mined for the larger social ideals that shape its notion of politics, social theory, and the role of educators and other cultural workers as engaged, public intellectuals. Freire's work demands critical scrutiny because it offers important theoretical and practical insights for rethinking the purpose of schooling and the political implications of cultural education as part of a broader struggle for freedom and democracy.

ERASING SCHOOLING AS AN OPPOSITIONAL PUBLIC SPHERE

As progressive institutions, American schools often have been viewed as democratic public spheres where students could learn how to master the capacities for critical consciousness, learn how to engage in public debate, and alter structures of power that shaped their identity and social existence.[16] Schooling and politics seen from this perspective linked the operations of power and authority to the logic of freedom and the imperatives of hope for generations of young people. Grounded in democratic social relations and oppositional knowledge that revealed new possibilities for the wider revitalization of public life, hope, and social vision provided the fundamental conditions that made critical education necessary and politics possible.

Commentators from Thomas Jefferson, to Horace Mann, to John Dewey recognized in different ways that schooling must be understood within the broader social, political, and economic considerations that shape the larger society.[17] Liberals and conservatives alike often saw public schools as vital to the life of the nation, although in different ways. Liberals claimed that schools were essential for giving students the knowledge and skills they needed to become critical citizens. Conservatives, on the other hand, often argued that public schools should educate students to be efficient and productive workers. As different as these views were, both camps believed that schools should be viewed as a public good.[18] Remarkably, often the test of the deeply-rooted assumption that schools are a public good found expression in the call for schools to solve recurrent "crises" and conflicts that mirrored society's most pressing problems. For example, the Little Rock crisis in the 1950s signaled the struggle for national desegregation following the Supreme Court's landmark 1954 decision in Brown v. Board of Education, which argued that separate schools for black and white children were inherently unequal. Since that decision, public schools have been the focus of an endless series of struggles manifested in the form of national "crises." A brief list of such crises include: the struggle over school decentralization in the nation's inner cites; the panic over Sputnik and the rush to educate students in order for the United States to win the space race and Cold War; the threat of Balkanization and the call for the schools to teach a common culture; the ongoing struggles by conservatives to organize schools along corporate models in order to meet the challenge of Japanese economic competition in the new global world order.

As contested sites, public schools provided a critical referent for a politics of the everyday in which the link between knowledge and power as well as between learning and social responsibility became meaningful as part of a broader reconstruction of democratic life. It was in the public schools that power, authority, and values clashed most visibly as it became clear that all educational practices presuppose some vision of the future and that all forms of teaching are based on exclusionary principles and represent particular ways of organizing the present and preparing students for the future. In the final analysis, the battle over schooling was part of a wider struggle over ideology, culture, the securing of specific forms of authority, and the legitimation of a regulated national identity. To be sure, behind the veil of innocence and democratic goodwill, schools largely showed preference to those who were white, male, and wealthy. But in spite of its repressive functions, dominant power proved leaky in its attempt to organize schools as agents of social and cultural reproduction. Schools were also about resistance, contradictions, and hope. In other words, public schools embodied both dominant ideologies and the possibility of resistance and struggle, and they were defended by diverse groups as fundamental for preparing students to assume the responsibilities of expanding the horizons of democracy and critical citizenship.[19]

Since the election of Ronald Reagan to the presidency in the 1980s and the expansion of neo-conservative control over the apparatuses of local, state, and national government, the debate about the nature and purpose of public schooling has changed dramatically. Public schools are no longer assumed to be important social and cultural sites through which to address various crises that affect the exercise of justice and equality. Nor are they viewed as essential to the reconstruction of democratic public life. In fact, as I pointed out in chapter 3, the very presence and legacy of schools as public spheres essential for educating students to be responsible and critical citizens is seen as either a threat by advocates of privatization or is scorned by conservatives as largely irrelevant since the school's intellectual and political mission has been largely subsumed by the corporate sector of society. By calling into question the link between schooling and justice, conservatives have largely redefined the role of public education. Public schools along with healthcare and social services are now defined as both troubled and troubling; in effect, schools, as key elements of the welfare state that provide an important resource for the reproduction of at least a semblance of democratic life, are labeled by many conservatives and liberals as the source of society's most pressing problems.[20]

Simultaneous with the dismantling of the welfare state, cutbacks in job programs, and the rise of anti-immigrant policies, education nationwide has experienced draconian cuts in federal aid that have undermined its ability to provide adequate resources and institutional support. This is especially the case in public schools in urban centers.[21] As public schools lose their financial base, systemically reduce teachers' skills, and disproportionately warehouse students who are poor and racially marginalized, they increasingly come under the ideological influence of corporate forces. Such schools face more than the absurd criticisms that they undermine Western values, promote a damaging identity politics, and subvert moral character through the teaching of sex education; they are also under attack by a number of aggressive right-wing conservatives who argue that public schools along with other public goods should be privatized and subject to market forms of regulation and organization.

Within the new right-wing discourse on schooling, questions of excellence have been abstracted from issues of equity. At the same time, any reference to educating students for critical citizenship and civic courage has been mortgaged to the dictates of the marketplace and virtually eliminated in the call for vouchers and the celebration of individual choice. Schools now offer corporations new markets for advertising their wares as part of a broader effort to transform youth into subjects who simply buy goods rather than critical subjects actively participating in all aspects of social life.[22] A call has arisen to replace public education with privately based educational institutions that can safely ignore civil rights, exclude students who are class and racially disenfranchised, and conveniently blur the lines between religion and the state.

TOWARD A POLITICS OF HOPE

Paulo Freire's life and work provide a valuable resource to challenge the ascendancy of the industrial model of corporate education and its "flagrant violation of the democratic educational mission."[23] Freire's belief in democratic schooling coupled with his faith in the ability of people to resist and transform oppressive institutions and ideologies has been forged in a spirit of struggle tempered by both the grim realities of his own imprisonment in Brazil and eventual exile in Geneva, Switzerland and a profound sense of humility, compassion, and hope. Acutely aware that many contemporary versions of hope were not anchored in practice and lacked a historical concreteness, Freire repeatedly denounced such romantic fantasies and was passionate about recovering and rearticulating hope through, in his words, an "understanding of history as opportunity and not determinism."[24]

Hope for Freire is a practice of witnessing, an act of moral imagination that encourages progressive educators to stand at the edge of society, to think beyond existing configurations of power in order to imagine the unthinkable in terms of how they might live with dignity, justice, and freedom. Hope, for Freire is not messianic, but strategic, born out of the ongoing contradictions that mark all societies. Hope demands an anchoring in transformative practices, and one of the tasks of progressive educators is to "unveil opportunities for hope, no matter what the obstacles may be."[25]

Underlying Freire's politics of hope is a view of radical education that locates itself on the dividing lines where the relations between domination and oppression, power and powerlessness continue to be produced and reproduced. Freire argues that radical democracy demands the ongoing production and struggle over knowledge, skills, values, and social relations in order to develop dynamic educational practices that are faithful to the spirit of open and democratic forms of insurgent citizenship. A radical educational process, in part, means listening to and working with the poor, oppressed, and other subordinate groups so that they might speak and act in order to change the concrete material and social conditions that exploit and oppress them.

Freire's politics of hope is grounded in a project that refuses the sectarianism of both the orthodox left and the authoritarianism of a backward-looking conservatism. According to Freire, material oppression and the affective investments that tie oppressed groups to the logic of domination cannot be grasped in all of their complexity within the singular logic of class struggle.[26] Moreover, the mechanisms of domination, both economic and ideological, cannot be understood without considering how the oppressed in many instances actually participate in their own oppression. As sociologist Stanley Aronowitz pointed out, Freire recognizes that "the oppressed are situated within an economic and social structure and tied to it not only by their labor but also by the conditions of their psychological being."[27]

For Freire, the prophetic nature of politics and education lies in a generalized notion of emancipation, one that recognizes the multiple forms of material, ideological, and psychological oppression at work in society. But unlike the poststructuralist tendency to translate diverse forms of class, race, and gender-based oppression to the discursive space of "subject positions," Freire refuses to separate the politics of representation from systemic relations of power. In this sense, Freire's commitment to Marxism is tempered by his commitment to the critical traditions of liberation theology, Freudianism, existentialism, radical humanism, and the more open Marxism of Antonio Gramsci and Amilcar Cabral.

MAKING THE EDUCATIONAL MORE POLITICAL

The role of an educator who is pedagogically and critically radical is to avoid being indifferent. . . . On the contrary, a better way to proceed is to assume the authority as a teacher whose direction of education

includes helping learners get involved in planning education, helping them create the critical capacity to
consider and participate in the direction and dreams of
education, rather than merely following blindly.

—Paulo Freire and Donaldo Macedo,
"A Dialogue: Culture, Language and Race"

Unfortunately, many of Freire's followers have reduced his educational theory to a methodology or set of teaching techniques
emphasizing dialogue, the affirmation of student experience, and
the decentralization of power in the classroom.[28] What has been
lost in this analysis is Freire's legacy of revolutionary politics. For
Freire, *problem-posing education* suggests not a methodology but a
social theory whose aim is the liberation of individuals and groups
as historical subjects through a critical educational process that
involves making the pedagogical more political and the political
more pedagogical. For Freire pedagogy is political in that its task is
to revitalize questions of individual and social agency as well as to
critically examine how power is produced, applied, and resisted
across a range of histories, social formations, institutions, and
signifying practices.

Education, according to Freire, is not concerned simply with
self-improvement but with social transformation aimed at creating
the conditions for the oppressed to overcome material, ideological,
and psychological forms of domination while reviving and expanding the fabric of democratic institutions. In this view, education and
politics mutually inform each other as part of a broader project that
requires addressing citizenship as "a social invention that demands
a certain political knowledge, a knowledge born of the struggle for
and the reflection on citizenship itself."[29] Freire's call for political
self-determination and for the oppressed to become agents not only
expresses a move away from a certain vanguardism—a hierarchical
and elitist notion of leadership—that marked his early work but
signals the need for educators to address the vast range of experi-

ences that inform the values and histories that students bring with them to the classroom and other educational sites. According to Freire, critical educators must always be attentive to the specific and the contingent; one of their primary undertakings is to recover and rethink the ways in which culture is related to power and how and where it functions both symbolically and institutionally as an educational, political, and economic force. For Freire, culture and power must be organized through an understanding of how the political becomes pedagogical—that is, how the very processes of learning constitute the political mechanisms through which identities are shaped, desires are mobilized, and experiences take on form and meaning. Pedagogy in this sense becomes central to the task of making knowledge meaningful in order to make it critical and transformative. For Freire, pedagogy is always the outcome of struggles that are historically specific, and "the sites, goals, and forms of struggle must be understood contextually."[30] Such struggles are defined by social issues and political projects that cannot be given beforehand; they emerge in response to specific formations and problems addressing where people are, how they actually live their lives, and what it might mean to open up "new imagined possibilities for changing [such] contexts."[31] Echoing Antonio Gramsci's insight that "Every relationship of 'hegemony' is necessarily an educational relationship,"[32] Freire reminds us that education takes place in multiple sites and he also signals how students and others are constructed as subjects and subjected to relations of power within and across a variety of public spaces.

Freire consistently informs us that political struggles are won and lost in those spaces that link narratives of everyday experience with the social gravity and material force of institutional power. Any radical educational approach that calls itself Freirean has to acknowledge the centrality of the particular and contingent in shaping historical contexts and political projects. Always taking seriously what it means to link political struggle with the contexts that give rise to pressing social problems, Freire develops educational practices forged in the struggles he addresses. For Freire, politics is about the making and the changing of contexts, and education is not simply the practical application of such politics but a performative struggle in which teaching and learning reflect the need for subordinate and marginalized groups to develop their languages, histories, and cultures in order to shape their own sense of political and cultural agency.

Committed to the specific and contextual, Freire offers no recipes for those in need of instant theoretical and political fixes. Nor does he wish to affirm and romanticize the experiences of students or subordinate groups. Freire refused either to reduce knowledge and politics to biography or to idealize marginality. More important, pedagogy is strategic and, at its best, moves beyond simply detailing models of domination and resistance by providing a discourse and politics of articulation and transformation. Considered as part of a broader political practice for democratic change, radical pedagogies cannot be viewed as an a priori discourse to be reasserted, a methodology to be implemented, or a mantra to uncritically affirm the voices of the oppressed. On the contrary, for Freire education is a theoretically rigorous, political, and performative act organized around the "instructive ambivalence of disrupted borders,"[33] a practice of bafflement, interruption, and intervention that is the result of ongoing historical, social, and economic struggles.

In Freire's radical educational theory, critical teaching practice means shifting power from the teacher to the students. Rather than suggesting that radical educators abandon authority, however, Freire calls upon them to assert authority in the service of creating a participatory and democratic classroom in which they provide exposition and explanation as a central feature of classroom dialogue and critique. Teachers become the "other" in this perspective, encouraging students to think beyond the conventions of common sense, to expand the horizons of what they know, and to develop a critical consciousness, rather than simply learning how to think critically. Critical consciousness suggests learning how to theorize, think relationally, and draw judgments based on evidence and a thorough understanding of events. Critical thinking is of a lesser order and refers more to the mastery of specific skills, techniques, and methods. Critical consciousness provides the opportunity for students to engage the formative nature of their own learning and what it means to appropriate education as a critical function. Crucial here is the recognition that while the teacher "is an actor on the social and political stage, the educator's task is to encourage human agency, not mold it in the manner of Pygmalion."[34] At the same time, Freire shuns the role of the educator as facilitator who turns all authority over to students, an educator who by default becomes silent in the face of injustice.

Freire also rejects using the authority of the teacher to collapse the political into the personal and rejects confusing the radical pedagogy with merely compassionate teaching: "What is taught is unproblematic; the only issue is how to teach on the basis of caring." The purpose of teacher authority in this anti-Frierian approach is to provide students with forms of therapy that focus largely on uplifting their self-esteem, motivating them, and making them feel good. Education for Freire was never simply a tool for student motivation or defined as a therapeutic tool to make students happy. On the contrary, the purpose of dialogue was individual and social change; its goal was not personal affirmation. Moreover, when classroom authority is reduced to a form of emotional uplift— transposing an all-knowing teacher against a victimized, vulnerable student—it represents for Freire "the false generosity of the oppressor."[35] Freire argues against the exercise of teacher authority in the service of an educational model that positions students as fragile, delicate victims of the dominant culture "in need of protection."[36] Drawing in part on the work of Freire, Lauren Berlant, English professor at the University of Chicago, brilliantly captures some of the political and educational problems generated by the therapeutic model when employed in some versions of feminist education. The idea of "false generosity" has become so prevalent in the appropriation of Freire's work that I want to elaborate on its implications by quoting Berlant's critique of this position at length.

> This very iconization of the teacher's power to make things possible leads constantly and incoherently to puzzlement, exhaustion, and feelings of domination, isolation, and abandonment for students and teachers both. Deep in the ambitions and socialization of the feminist teacher . . . is the promise . . . to make learning personal, socially transformative, and generationally supportive. This desire still inspires workers in the university system to make themselves vulnerable to the impossible higher expectations about institutionally and intellectually mediated personal relations that are hardwired into the feminist pedagogical project. It motivates taking on kinds of therapeutic and mentoring functions that are way beyond our expertise; it motivates us to over identify with students' happiness or unhappiness as the source of our value; it motivates the ways we shield students from experiencing the various kinds of ambivalence we have toward being called to personhood in this way.[37]

For Freire, educators have an obligation to dream and work with their students in order to create the conditions necessary to live, as he puts it, in "a world that is less oppressive and more humane toward the oppressed."[38] Radical educators also have a responsibility to present students with critical choices about the places they might inhabit in the larger society.

Freire forcefully acknowledges that educators can never impose their views on students or, as he puts it, "transform the learners' presence into a shadow of the educator's presence."[39] But this should not be seen as merely a defense of teaching multiple perspectives or as an endorsement of what English professor Gerald Graff refers to as teaching the conflicts.[40] On the contrary, Freire argues that educators must develop critical teaching practices grounded in existing concrete realities and social problems, and exhibit for students "an active presence in educational practice."[41] According to Freire, educators must fashion their educational practices within a democratic social project and seize authority in order "to stimulate learners to live a critically conscious presence in the pedagogical and historical process."[42] In this project, the role of the educator is directive and theoretically informed. Critical educators cannot impose their views on students by telling them what to think, but they can "teach them the importance of taking a stance that is rooted in rigorous engagement with the full range of ideas about a topic"[43] while stressing the social and not merely individualistic character of learning and struggle.

Freire's radical education insists that learners become a subject in their own education by critically engaging through dialogue and debate the historical, social, and economic conditions that both limit and enable their own understanding of knowledge as power. According to Freire, engaging authority critically cannot be justified in exclusively methodological terms as in a call to teach conflicts or simply to participate in dialogue. In exercising and defending teacher authority, educators must be able to name their own location, openly articulate their project and vision, reveal their partialities, refuse to silence students, and open their own meaning and use of authority to critical debate.

It is impossible to be faithful to the spirit of Paulo Freire's work without recognizing what an "old-fashioned" modernist he is. He cannot imagine a politics without subjects, hope, justice, and the need to take a position without being doctrinaire. But at the same time, he takes the postmodern turn seriously when it highlights the changing nature of difference, the powerful role that electronically mediated culture plays in shaping identities, and the importance of the changing nature of the production of knowledge in the age of computer-based technologies. Combining the modernist emphasis on justice and emancipation with a postmodern critique of master narratives, his view of authority is one of his lasting contributions to critical theory. Rather than run away from the burden and politics of authority, he gives it an emancipatory register and relentlessly defends the position that any form of critical education that simply equates authority with domination is part of the problem. Authority is central to politics, and it must be fused with the language and practice of freedom.

Freire also challenges the separation of culture from politics by calling attention to how diverse technologies of power work within institutions to produce, regulate, and legitimate particular forms of knowing, belonging, feeling, and desiring. But Freire does not make the mistake of many of his contemporaries by conflating culture with the politics of language and meaning. Politics is more than a gesture of translation, representation, and dialogue. Politics is also about mobilizing social movements against the oppressive economic, racial, and sexist practices put into place by colonization, global capitalism, and other structures of power. A critical theory of literacy and culture is central to Freire's radical educational project, but literacy and culture cannot be understood outside of the equally important registers of the material economy of power, resources, and means. Freire repeatedly emphasizes culture as an important site of political struggle, but he also insists that if such a sphere is to have any radical educational relevance, students and educators must assess it critically so that they can intervene in the material circumstances that have shaped their lives. For Freire, a cultural politics that lacks a historical dimension or ignores the machinations of power that shape the relations among schools, everyday life, and speech fails to address the revolutionary potential of critical education and undermines the project of social reconstruction.

Paulo Freire's corpus of work emerged from a lifetime of struggle and commitment. His work is always unsettled and unsettling, restless yet engaging. Unlike so much of the politically arid and morally vacuous academic and public prose that characterizes much of contemporary educational discourse, Freire's work is consistently fueled by a healthy rage over the needless oppression and suffering he witnessed during his worldwide travels. His work exhibits a vibrant and dynamic quality that allows it to grow, to refuse easy formulas, and to open itself to new political realities and projects. Freire elaborated a theory of social change and engagement that was neither elitist nor populist. He had a profound faith in the ability of ordinary people to become critical agents in shaping history, but he also refused to romanticize the culture and experiences of those who bore the weight of oppressive social conditions. Combining theoretical rigor, social relevance, and moral compassion, Freire's work and politics give new meaning to the registers of daily life while affirming the importance of critical theory and radical education to open up the space of critique, possibility, and practice. Theory and language are tools of struggle and possibility that give experience meaning and action a political direction, and Friere repeatedly condemned any attempt to reproduce the binary division of theory and politics.[44]

The issues that Freire explores in his educational theory and practice have enormous relevance for how educators and other progressives define the role of the public school, make education a defining principle of politics, and assert the importance of schools as democratic public spheres. At a time when public education is being either eliminated or vocationalized it becomes all the more crucial for educators to defend it as one of the few places left where democracy can be experienced or at least acknowledged as central to educating students for the future. Freire's passionate defense of radical democracy provides a crucial resource for critical educators and other progressives to reclaim public education as a site of democratic education and struggle. Against the elitism of conservatives Allan Bloom, William Bennett, Diane Ravitch, and E. D. Hirsch, Freire offers a passionate defense of popular culture as an educational starting point for developing multiple vocabularies and literacies that enable people to negotiate the public realm, take seriously the imperatives of creating a transnational democracy, and expand individual and collective capacities for social engagement. Freire never abstracts his methods from a larger vision of freedom; nor does he relent in his advocacy for an international sense of responsibility. He offers his readers a language of critique and possibility that calls for a new collective subject, constituted across multiple borders and willing to fight and struggle for social change.

Freire's untimely death in 1997 unfolds against a legacy that embraces him as a grand figure who had a wonderful sense of life and a passion for living.[45] Life was too beautiful for him to not share its wealth and benefits with others. Freire's presence in the world turned poetry into politics and humility into a requisite for political engagement; he never reduced the suffering of others to his own desires, needs, or politics. Moral righteousness was not part of his script. Perhaps that is why he was able to speak to so many different people with such compassion and love. He was attentive to others without being self-serving, committed to eliminating oppression but not self-righteous about his role in doing so; he was politically committed but well aware of the complexity of struggle and cognizant that complex social issues could not be reduced to a set of prescribed activities.

SIX

Stuart Hall and the Politics of Education

> We all want to do the very best for our children. But
> what is education if it is not the process by which society
> inculcates its norms, standards and values—in short, its
> "culture"—into the next generation in the hope and
> expectation that, in this way, it will broadly guide,
> channel, influence and shape the actions and beliefs of
> future generations in line with the values and norms of
> its parents and the prevailing value-system of society?
> What is this if not regulation—moral governance by
> culture?
>
> —Stuart Hall, "Centrality of Culture:
> Notes on the Cultural Revolutions of Our Time"
> in *Media and Cultural Regulation*

INTRODUCTION

Over the last forty years, Stuart Hall, the prominent British cultural
studies theorist, has produced an impressive body of work on the
relationship between culture and power, and culture's formative
role as a political and educational practice produced and mediated
within different social contexts, spatial relations, and historical
conjectures.[1] Refusing to confine culture to narrow epistemological

categories, the exclusive study of texts, or to matters of taste, Hall argues that cultural power is what distinguishes cultural studies from other disciplines and academic areas.[2] Cultural politics in his view "combin[es] the study of symbolic forms and meanings with the study of power," or more specifically what he calls the "insertion of symbolic processes into societal contexts and their imbrication with power."[3] According to Hall, culture is central to understanding struggles over meaning, identity, and power. He has written extensively on the importance of the political force of culture and the diverse ways in which culture deploys power to shape identities and subjectivities within a circuit of practices that range from the production and distribution of goods and representations to an ever growing emphasis on regulation and consumption.[4]

Hall's work provides an important framework for making pedagogy central to the theory and practice of cultural politics. His work is also crucial for understanding pedagogy as a mode of cultural criticism that is essential for questioning the conditions under which knowledge is produced and subject positions are put into place, negotiated, taken up, or refused.[5] Hall also offers a critical and strategic challenge to the backlash against pedagogy and the politics of culture that has emerged in the United States by ideologues as different as English professor Harold Bloom, philosopher Richard Rorty, and sociologist Todd Gitlin.[6] Essential to this debate is not simply the issue of how we think of politics, understand the dynamics of culture within the shifting discursive practices and material relations of power, but also how we can, as cultural theorist Larry Grossberg suggests, "inquire into the conditions of the possibility of agency."[7] For theorists such as Hall and Grossberg, culture is a strategic pedagogical and political terrain whose force as a "crucial site and weapon of power in the modern world"[8] can, in part, be understood in its contextual specificity. That specificity can be engaged only in relation to broader public discourses and practices whose meaning is to be found in culture's articulation with other sites, contexts, and social practices.

In what follows, I argue that Hall's attention to the relationship between culture and politics provides a valuable service to educators by contributing to a notion of public pedagogy that makes the pedagogical a defining principle of cultural politics. Moreover, Hall's work amplifies the role that educators might play as public intellectuals working in diverse sites and projects to expand the possibilities for democratic struggles and social transformation. For Hall, such struggles are not predefined; rather they rest on the ethical and political imperative to find and use "the intellectual resources in order to understand [and transform] what keeps making the lives we live, and the societies we live in, profoundly and deeply antihumane in the capacity to live with difference."[9] But before I take up some of Hall's contributions to a politics of public education, I want to discuss the recent attack on education and cultural politics that has cut across ideological lines. I also examine how such arguments undermine the possibility of making the political more pedagogical as part of a broader democratic project for radical social change. Hall's work provides an important theoretical and political corrective to these discussions. I conclude by exploring the implications of Hall's writings for those of us who believe that pedagogy is central to any notion of radical cultural politics and the development of cultural politics is a crucial precondition for understanding the struggle over meaning, power, and identities in public spheres such as public and higher education.

SCHOOLING WITHOUT POLITICS?

What is surprising about the current attack on education, especially in light of growing commercialization and privatization, is the refusal of many theorists to rethink the role academics might play in utilizing the university (and public schooling) as a crucial public sphere. This public sphere would foster new notions of civic courage and action and it would address what it means to make the pedagogical more political in a time of growing conservatism, racism, and corporatism. Even more surprising is the common ground shared by a growing number of progressives and conservatives on basic educational issues. The seduction of methodological quick fixes—in which pedagogy is reduced to techniques or instrumentalized accountability schemes—has long plagued educators across ideological lines. More recently, however, the controversy over cultural politics has generated resentment from right and left intellectuals alike.

For conservatives such as Harold Bloom, Lynn Chaney, Chester Finn, Jr., and William Bennett, culture has no politics; it is the repository of beauty and transcendent values, and the bearer of the most sacred traditions of Western civilization. Conservatives often denounce any notion of politics that questions this select reading of culture and its ethnocentric bias as simply a version of "political correctness."[10] In this perspective, culture serves as a figure of speech to separate knowledge from power and to reduce the university's role to the imperative of teaching the "best that has been thought and known in the world."[11] But the attack on cultural politics and the role it plays as an educational and political force is no longer limited to conservatives but evident also in the works of a number of progressives. Unlike conservative theorists, intellectuals such as Todd Gitlin, Michael Tomasky, and Jim Sleeper speak from the vantage point of left politics but display a similar contempt for cultural politics, popular culture, cultural pedagogy, and all notions of identity politics that embrace differences based on race, ethnicity, gender, and sexual orientation.[12]

Within this orthodox left/liberal discourse, contemporary cultural struggles, especially those taken up by social movements organized around sexuality, gender, race, the politics of representation, and, more broadly, multiculturalism, are considered to be nothing more than a weak substitute for "real-world" politics, notably one that focuses on class, labor, and economic inequality.[13] According to Gitlin, social movements that reject the primacy of class give politics a bad name because they serve mainly to splinter the left into identity sects, fail "to address questions of economic equity and redistribution,"[14] and offer no unifying vision of a common good capable of challenging corporate power and right-wing ideologues.

This analysis omits a history of left orthodoxy in which class politics was used to demean and domesticate the modalities of race, gender, and sexual orientation by denying the autonomy and political significance of these social forces and movements. Moreover, such movements developed independently of exclusive class-based politics precisely because of the subordination of different social groups that organized to articulate their respective goals, histories, and interests outside of the orthodoxy of class politics. Within this orthodox Marxist position, the history of class-based sectarianism is forgotten, the category of class is taken up reductively, and politics is so narrowly defined as to freeze the open-ended and shifting relationship between culture and power.[15] Moreover, as Stuart Hall points out, within this form of sectarian analysis it is impossible to understand how class is actually lived through everyday experiences that are shaped by race and gender. Moreover, such class-based criticism finds its antithesis in a version of cultural studies that is pure caricature. For example, Gitlin argues that cultural studies is a form of populism intent on finding resistance in the most mundane of cultural practices, ignoring the ever-deepening economic inequities, and dispensing entirely with material relations of power. Banal in its refusal to discriminate between a culture of excellence and consumer culture, cultural studies, in this perspective, becomes a symbol of bad faith and political irresponsibility. For theorists in cultural studies, Gitlin argues, it is irrelevant that African Americans suffer gross material injustice because what really matters is that "they have rap."[16] It seems that for Gitlin and his cohorts cultural studies should "free itself of the burden of imagining itself to be a political practice"[17] since much of its work is located in the university—a bankrupt site, according to Gitlin, for intellectuals to address the most pressing questions of our age. Rather than take responsibility for what Hall calls "translating knowledge into the practice of culture,"[18] academics, according to Gitlin, should put "real politics" ahead of cultural matters, "not mistake the academy for the larger world, [and] put their efforts into organizing groups, coalitions, and movements"[19] in order to address the most demanding problems caused by capitalistic inequalities.

These theorists denigrate social movements as merely cultural, and they dismiss the cultural as a serious terrain of political struggle. Unfortunately, this critique not only fails to recognize how issues of race, gender, age, sexual orientation, and class are intertwined, it also refuses to acknowledge the educational function of culture in constructing identities, mobilizing desires, and shaping moral values. Questions of agency and resistance in cultural studies are dismissed by the economistic left as retrograde forms of pedagogy, while cultural pedagogy is displaced by an anti-intellectual and antitheoretical incitement to organizing and pamphleteering.

What is disturbing about this position is that its proponents seem completely unaware of the complexity of views that characterize the field of cultural studies. This position makes no distinction between the diverse theoretical work being done in cultural studies in Australia, the United Kingdom, Canada, Latin America, and the United States. But there is more at work here than simply constructing a strawman; there is also a willful misrepresentation of what many cultural studies theorists actually do. Those who suggest that political economy is missing from the work of cultural studies theorists, or who argue that it simply romanticizes popular culture or reduces politics to questions of identity while flaunting the material and institutional nature of power, are completely ignorant of the scholarship being produced in the field.[20]

Moreover, many progressives who appropriate the left-wing orthodox attack on the merging of politics, culture, and power overlook the attempt by some cultural studies theorists to reassert the political and educational relevance of culture to social change.

Consequently, the so-called progressive alternative to cultural studies not only separates culture from politics, but it also leaves no room to capture the contradictions present in dominant institutions. Examining such contradictions opens up political and social possibilities for contesting domination, doing critical work within the schools and other public spheres, or furthering the capacity of students to question oppressive forms of authority and operations of power.

For instance, when social theorists such as Francis Mulhern suggest that cultural studies seeks to subordinate or subsume the meaning of the political into popular culture, he does more than misrepresent cultural studies, he unwittingly argues that where culture is merely educative, it is not deliberate and therefore not political.[21] This is a reckless theoretical move, one that fails to grasp the emergence of information as a new mode of production in the post-Fordist era. Witness to this transformation, Stuart Hall has argued for the centrality of culture in the formation of subjective and social identities.[22] As Hall points out, the intellectual turn to popular culture is about more than providing a connection between theory and the popular. On the contrary, the intellectual engagement with the popular "is not an indulgence and an affirmation; it's a political, intellectual, pedagogical commitment. Everybody now inhabits the popular, whether they like it or not, so that does create a set of common languages. To ignore the pedagogical possibilities of common languages is extremely political."[23] Mulhern has no vocabulary for examining the educational force of popular culture. Nor does he have any interest in understanding how pedagogical practices can be used to disrupt dominant forms of common sense and to provide alternative categories, maps of meaning, and a range of possibilities through which people might imagine and define themselves as social actors and discover their own political agency.

Arguments against the relevance of pedagogy in cultural politics are also present in the work of Australian educator, Ian

Hunter. In dismissing pedagogy as simply another instrument for reconciling the self with dominant society (what Hunter, borrowing from Foucault, calls governmentality), he rejects any possibility for fashioning forms of pedagogical practice that call critical attention to the ways in which authority might be used to undermine the social and cultural reproduction of the dominant ideologies and practices that characterize public spheres such as public schools and higher education. Reducing all pedagogy to the imposition of dominant authority, Hunter can only imagine pedagogical authority working in the interest of moral regulation and social control. Self-reflexive dialogue about academic labor drops out of his argument, as does the possibility of teachers and students becoming critical of the very institutional forms, academic relations, and regulating disciplines that constitute the complex and varied spaces of schooling. Within this narrow understanding of the relationship between culture and politics, there is no possibility for imagining schools as a place to resist dominant authority, to unsettle the complacency of strategies of domination, or for educators to re-elaborate institutional authority from a position of engaged criticism. That the legacy of such cultural regulation can be challenged, turned in on itself, or used as a resource to refigure the basis of teaching as a deliberative practice in the service of a progressive cultural politics seems impossible to these theorists.[24]

I am not suggesting that institutional practices forged within dominant economic, cultural, and political conditions do not exercise enormous force in shaping the very conditions under which education takes place. But to acknowledge the latter, as cultural studies theorist Alan O'Shea has pointed out, does not legitimate the presupposition that power is entirely on the side of domination within schools, that teachers and students can only be complicitous with dominant forms of power, however they may challenge its structures, ideologies, and practices.[25] Within this updated model of social and moral reproduction, critique and contestation can come only from outside of institutional schooling, offered up by cultural critics "uncontaminated" by the moral technologies such institutions impose on "hapless" reformers and radicals. Such criticism rests on more than passé functionalist accounts of society and its social forms; it also legitimates a totalizing model of power that marks a retreat from making the political more pedagogical as it simultaneously celebrates the marginalized role of the detached critic. This represents more than the exhaustion of a bad version of Foucauldian politics; it also signals a form of theoretical paralysis (not simply anti-utopianism) that undermines the more crucial problem of how culture as a terrain of struggle functions educationally to shape the possibilities of political agency and critical engagement within dominant cultural and institutional forms. Lost here is any critical attentiveness to how teachers and students might construct and mediate educational authority as a form of self-critique or as a response to the particular histories, institutional formations, and cultural forces that bear down on the sites in which they teach and learn. This version of political power and control has no language for understanding pedagogy as the outgrowth of specific struggles that take place within varied contexts marked by unequal relations of power, differentiated opportunities for resistance, and varied resources for social transformation. In this discourse, pedagogy has no role in critically engaging ongoing public conversations about crucial social and political issues.

Stuart Hall's work provides an important theoretical and political service in face of the current onslaught against cultural politics and the attempts to discredit the role that educators might play as public intellectuals working in a diverse range of public spheres that extend from the university to the mass media. In what follows, I want to focus on some important elements in Hall's work that constitute what I loosely call a theory of critical public pedagogy.

STRUGGLING OVER CULTURE

For Hall, culture provides the constitutive framework for making the pedagogical political—recognizing that how we come to learn and what we learn is immanently tied to strategies of understanding, representation, and disruption. These strategies offer opportunities for individuals to engage and transform when necessary the ideological and material circumstances that shape their lives. One of Hall's lasting contributions also has been to make the political more pedagogical. By repeatedly pointing to the various ways in which culture is related to power and how and where culture functions both symbolically and institutionally as an educational, political, and economic force, Hall argues that cultural pedagogy is the outcome of particular struggles over specific representations, identifications, and forms of agency. Both the urgency and relevance of such struggles become more clear when defining questions of identities and identifications. Such questions are defined, in Hall's words, by "using the resources of history, language and culture in the process of becoming rather than being: not 'who we are' or 'where we came from' so much as what we might become, how we have been represented and how that bears on how we might represent ourselves."[26]

To Hall, public pedagogy as a struggle over identifications is crucial to raising broader questions about how notions of difference, civic responsibility, community, and belonging are produced "in specific historical and institutional sites within specific discursive formations and practices, by specific enunciative strategies."[27] Such strategies are organized not only around how meaning is theorized but also around the struggle implied in what Hall has recently called the "governing of culture."[28] By this term he means the struggle over the control, regulation, and distribution of resources that mediate the range of capacities and possibilities that enable individuals and social groups to choose, inhabit, and transform particular notions of identity, desire, and agency. Cultural politics, for Hall, is in part about the regulation and distribution of resources. But our capacity to think politics is also mediated by the ways in which culture actually governs, the ways in which it shapes "our conduct, social action, human practices and thus the way people act within institutions and in society at large." Our capacity to think politics is also dependent on the ways it establishes the terrain "through which boundaries mark differences as potential sites of contestation over meaning, a politics of identity."[29] In short, culture is constitutive of agency(ies) and politics because it provides the resources through which individuals learn how to relate to themselves, others, and the world around them.

For Hall, culture is neither free-floating nor unmoving. But Hall does more than acknowledge that culture is a terrain of struggle. Throughout his career, he has insisted that cultural workers deepen the meaning of the political by producing educational practices that engage and challenge those representational strategies, institutional forms, and technologies of power that condition and are conditioned by the indeterminate play of power, conflict, and oppression within society. Culture is the social field where power repeatedly mutates, where identities are shaped but always in transit, and where agency is often located where it is least acknowledged. Agency in this discourse is neither prefigured nor always in place but is subject to negotiation. Agency offers hope and a site of struggle for integrating work, play, life, and desire within democratic practices and structures. How one "deals with the place of cultural politics" remains essential to any viable notion of politics concerned with how individuals and social groups re-examine the role that existing educational forces play in the maintenance of dominant relations of power.[30]

For Hall, the educational force of culture resides in the attention it pays to representations and ethical discourses as the very conditions for learning, agency, the functioning of social practices, and politics itself. Culture gives meaning to the forms, shapes, and practices through which people live their everyday existences. As an educational force, culture is saturated with politics. In the broadest sense, culture offers both the symbolic and the material resources as well as the context and content needed for the negotiation of knowledge and skills. Through this negotiation, culture enables a critical reading of the world from a position of agency and possibility, although within unequal relations of power. The changing nature of the representations, space, and institutions of culture in modern times is central to an understanding of its educational function. On one hand, culture is substantive in that as a complex of institutions, new technologies, practices, and products it has vastly expanded "the scope, volume, and variety of meanings, messages, and images that can be transmitted" through time and space.[31] On the other hand, the explosion of information produced within the cultural realm registers the shift in thinking about knowledge as a primary form of production, if not the key productive force. Culture in these terms is more than "either a text or a commodity," it is the site "of the production and struggle over power."[32] Culture's primacy as a substantive and epistemological force highlights its educational nature as a site where identities are continually being transformed and power enacted. Within this context, learning itself becomes the means not only for the acquisition of agency but for the concept of social change itself.

CULTURE AS PUBLIC PEDAGOGY

According to Hall, the educational force of culture redefines the politics of power, the political nature of representation, and the centrality of education as a defining principle of social change; it also expands our understanding of the public impact of pedagogy as an educational practice that "operates both inside and outside the academy,"[33] expanding its reach across multiple sites and spheres. As a performative practice, pedagogy is at work in all of those public spaces where culture works to secure identities; it does the bridging work for negotiating the relationship among knowledge, pleasure, and values; and it renders authority both crucial and problematic in legitimating particular social practices, communities, and forms of power. It is precisely this legacy of both politicizing culture and insisting on the pedagogical nature of the political that makes Hall's work so important at the present time. If agency is negotiated, made and remade within the symbolic and material relations of power, and enacted within diverse and changing historical and relational contexts, it cannot be removed from the self-reflexive possibilities of education; nor can it be removed from the dynamics of cultural politics.

Hall's theory of articulation is of considerable importance to critical educators when analyzing how authority and power actually work in linking texts to contexts, ideology to specific relations of power, and political projects to existing social formations.[34] For educators this is an important insight that points to the centrality of context in shaping cultural pedagogy as a form of practical politics. Not only do political projects emerge out of particular contexts, but because contexts change as the relations between culture and power shift, such projects become practical only if they remain open, partial, and incomplete. Central to Hall's work is the insight that public pedagogy is defined through its performative functions, its ongoing work of mediation, and its attentiveness to the interconnections and struggles that take place concerning knowledge, language, spatial relations, and history. Public pedagogy for Hall represents a moral and political practice rather than merely a technical procedure. At stake here is not only the call to link public pedagogy to practices that are interdisciplinary, transgressive, and oppositional, but also to connect such practices to broader projects designed to further racial, economic, and political democracy, to strike a new balance and expand what Stuart Hall and David Held have called the "individual and social dimensions of citizenship rights."[35]

The concept of articulation does more than provide a theoretical rationale for "the making of a relationship out of a nonrelationship or, more often, the making of one relationship out of another one."[36] Articulation also reaffirms the political nature of cultural work, giving meaning to the resources that students bring with them to various sites of learning while simultaneously subjecting the specificities of such meanings to broader interrogations and public dialogue. This is a crucial concept for any notion of public pedagogy. Central to such a project is the need to begin at those intersections where people actually live their lives and where meaning is produced, assumed, and contested in the unequal relations of power that construct the mundane acts of everyday relations. Public pedagogy in this context becomes part of a critical practice designed to understand the social context of everyday life as lived relations of power.

Hall has consistently insisted that cultural workers must critically examine how meanings work to resonate with ideologies that are produced in other sites. Cultural workers must also examine how meanings work to legitimate and produce particular practices, policies, and social relations. Educators cannot treat cultural texts as if they were hermetic or pure; such approaches often ignore how representations are linked to wider social forms, power, and public struggles. Engaging cultural texts as a form of public pedagogy means refusing to limit our analysis of popular texts by focusing on the polyphonic meanings at work in such texts or by employing formalist strategies to decipher what is perceived as a text's preferred meanings. On the contrary, a critical public pedagogy should ascertain how certain meanings under particular historical conditions become more legitimate as representations of reality and take on the force of commonsense assumptions shaping a broader set of discourses and social configurations at work in the dominant social order. Hall's work emphasizes the need for educators to focus on representations as a mode of public exchange in order to explore, as cultural critic Herman Gray attests, the ways "these images, especially the historical and contemporary meanings they carry and understandings they express, are aligned and realigned with broader discourses."[37] As public discourses, representations can be understood for the ways in which they shape and bear witness to the ethical dilemmas that animate broader debates within the dominant culture. The implications of this argument suggest a cultural politics that investigates how popular texts are articulated within structures of affect and meaning mediated by networks of power and domination bound to the specific historical, social and economic conditions of their production.

PUBLIC PEDAGOGY AS POLITICS

I have argued that Hall's work supports a notion of public pedagogy that is interdisciplinary in its continual involvement in border crossings, transgressive in its challenge to authority and power, and intertextual in its attempt to link the specific with the national and transnational. The project underlying such pedagogical strategies may take many forms, but its deepest impulse is rooted in issues of compassion and social responsibility aimed at deepening and extending the possibilities for critical agency, racial justice, and economic and political democracy.

Stuart Hall's work is refreshingly theoretical, contextual, and rigorous: It is accessible but refuses easy answers. But most important, Hall attempts to make hope practical and social justice the foundation of his cultural politics and pedagogy. Hall's work both instructs and disrupts, opens a dialogue but refuses rigid adherence to a position that closes down deliberation and reflection.

Finally, Hall's writing has always refused to limit the sites of education and politics to those "privileged" by the advocates of "genuine" politics. Organizing labor unions, demonstrating in the streets for legislation to curb corporate crimes, and organizing workers to promote radical forms of social policy are important forms of political practice, but working in the public schools, the television industry, law firms, museums, or a vast number of other public spheres does not constitute for Hall a less reputable or less important form of political work. In fact, Hall continually has called for intellectuals to "address the central, urgent, and most disturbing questions of a society and a culture in the most rigorous intellectual way we have available."[38] He has urged cultural workers to take up this challenge in a variety of educational sites, and in doing so he has opened the possibility for working within dominant institutions while challenging their authority and cultural practices. For Hall, the context of such work demands confronting a major paradox in capitalist societies—that of using the very authority vested in institutions such as schools to work against the grain of such authority. Such strategies are not a retreat from politics, as Gitlin and others believe, but an expansion of the possibility of politics and agency to the very institutions that work to shut down notions of critical consciousness and political action. Authority in this context struggles against the tendency to be complicitous and opens up the possibility of being resistant, transformative, and contestatory. This discourse locates public pedagogy and cultural politics "on the dividing lines where the relation between domination and subordination continues to be produced, lines that extend into the academy itself."[39] Hall's call for a cultural politics necessitates a public pedagogy in which learning becomes indispensable to the very process of social change and social change becomes the precondition for a politics that moves in the direction of a less hierarchical, more radical democratic social order.

NOTES

INTRODUCTION

1. The end of history theme was made famous in Francis Fukuyama, *The End of History and the Last Man* (New York: Free Press, 1992).
2. Marina Warner, *Six Myths of Our Time* (New York: Vintage, 1995), p. 56.
3. The universalized notion of childhood and innocence is dismantled in a range of historical work on childhood. See Philippe Aries, *Centuries of Childhood* (London: Cate Press, 1973, c. 1962); Chris Jenks, *Childhood* (New York: Routledge, 1996); Anne Higonnet, *Pictures of Innocence: The History and Crisis of Ideal Childhood* (New York: Thames and Hudson, 1998). For a history of contemporary youth cultures and history, see Joe Austin and Michael Nevin Willard, eds., *Generations of Youth* (New York: New York University Press, 1998). See also Paul Goodman, *Growing Up Absurd: Problems of Youth in the Organized System* (New York: Random House, 1960).
4. Edward W. Said, *Representations of the Intellectual* (New York: Pantheon, 1994), p.74.
5. Richard Johnson, "Reinventing Cultural Studies: Remembering for the Best Version," in Elizabeth Long, ed., *From Sociology to Cultural Studies* (Malden, Mass.: Basil Blackwell, 1997), p. 461.
6. See, for example, Harold Bloom, *The Western Canon* (New York: Riverhead Books, 1994). For a critique of this position, see Stanley Aronowitz and Henry A. Giroux, *Postmodern Education* (Minneapolis: University of Minnesota Press, 1991); and Lawrence Levine, *The Opening of the American Mind* (Boston: Beacon Press 1996); Stanley Aronowitz, *The Knowledge Factory* (Boston: Beacon Press, 2000).
7. Ibid., p. 122.
8. I want to emphasize that in using the general term "adults," I am not suggesting that the relationship between children and adults is defined generationally. On the contrary, while all adults are capable of abusing young people, the central issue of adult power cannot be abstracted from larger class, racial, and gender formations, nor can it be removed from the dynamics of American capitalism itself, which I believe should be at the forefront of any analysis of what many youth have to endure in the United States at the present time.
9. This national tragedy is captured by one national commission on youth when it acknowledges that "Never before has one generation of American children been less healthy, less cared for, or less prepared for life than their parents were at the same age." See National Commission on the Role of the Schools and the Community in Improving Adolescent Health, *Code Blue: Uniting for Healthier Youth* (Washington, D.C.: National Association of State Boards of Education/ American Medical Association, 1990), p. 3.

10. Lauren Berlant cited in Jenkins, "Introduction: Childhood Innocence and Other Myths," p. 11.

11. As Mike Males has pointed out, drug use and arrest for violent crimes among youth has declined significantly since 1995. See Mike Males, "Five Myths and Why Adults Believe They Are True," *New York Times* (April 29, 1998), p. 9. David Cole, *No Equal Justice: Race and Class in the American Criminal Justice System* (New York: The New Press, 1999). For a passionate and moving commentary on the plight children face when incarcerated with adults, see Anthony Lewis, "Suffer the Children," *New York Times,* July 7, 1997, p. A23.

12. Lauren Berlant, *The Queen of America Goes to Washington City* (Durham, N.C.: Duke University Press, 1997), p. 5.

13. Cited in Patricia J. Williams, "The Auguries of Innocence," *The Nation,* May 24, 1999, p. 9.

14. Ibid.

15. Cited in Courtland Milloy, "A Look at Tragedy in Black, White," *Washington Post,* May 2, 1999, p. CO1.

16. Orlando Patterson, "When 'They' Are 'Us,'" *New York Times,* April 30, 1999, p. A31.

17. For a brilliant and moving commentary on the changing politics and experience of youth in the 1980s, see Lawrence Grossberg, *We Gotta Get Outta Here* (New York: Routledge, 1992); also see William Finnegan, *Cold New World: Growing Up in a Harder Country* (New York: Random House, 1998); Angela McRobbie, *Postmodernism and Popular Culture* (New York: Routledge, 1994).

18. I have taken up this issue in Henry A. Giroux, *Fugitive Cultures: Race, Violence, and Youth* (New York: Routledge, 1996); Henry A. Giroux, *Channel Surfing: Racism, the Media and the Destruction of Today's Youth* (New York: St. Martin's Press, 1998).

19. This argument is taken up in Mike Males, *Framing Youth: 10 Myths About the Next Generation* (Monroe, Me: Common Courage Press, 1999).

20. Sharon Stephens, "Children and the Politics of Culture in 'Late Capitalism,'" in Sharon Stephens, ed., *Children and the Politics of Culture* (Princeton, N.J.: Princeton University Press, 1995), p. 13.

21. Cynthia Tucker, "In Littleton's Wake, We All Turn to Movies," *The Atlanta Constitution,* April 25, 1999, p. 5C.

22. Cited in Robin D. G. Kelley, *Yo' Mama's Disfunktional!: Fighting the Culture Wars in Urban America* (Boston: Beacon Press, 1997), p. 44.

23. Males, *Framing Youth,* p. 12.

24. Sharon Stephens ask a similar question: "What are the implications for society as a whole, if there are no longer social spaces conceived as at least partially autonomous from the market and market-driven politics? Where are we to find the sites of difference, the terrain of social witness, critical leverage and utopian vision, insofar as the domain of childhood—or of everyday life or of a semiautonomous realm of culture—is increasing shot through with the values of the marketplace and the discursive politics of postmodern global culture? And what happens to the bodies and minds of children in the process?" "Children and the Politics of Culture in 'Late Capitalism,'" p. 24.

25. Neil Postman, *The Disappearance of Childhood* (New York: Vintage Books, 1994); David Elkind, *The Hurried Child: Growing Up Too Fast Too Soon* (Reading, Mass.: Addison-Wesley, 1981); David Elkind, *Reinventing Childhood* (Rosemont: Modern Learning Press, 1998); David Elkind, "The Social Determination of Childhood and Adolescence," *Education Week,* February 24, 1998, pp. 48-50.

26. One almost hysterical tirade against student use of the Internet and videogames can be found in John Leland, "The Secret Life of Teens," *Newsweek,* May 10, 1999, pp. 45-50.

27. For an important commentary on the recent public attack on the new electronic media and its affect on youth, especially in light of the Littleton tragedy, see Henry Jenkins, "Testimony Before the U. S. Senate Committee," May 4, 1999.

28. David Elkind, "The Social Determination of Childhood and Adolescence," pp. 48-50.

29. Higonnet, *Pictures of Innocence*, p. 194.

30. Annette Fuentes, "The Crackdown on Kids," *The Nation*, June 15/22, 1998, p. 21.

31. Steve Farkas and Jean Johnson, *Kids These Days: What Americans Really Think About the Next Generation*, a report from Public Agenda, sponsored by Ronald McDonald House Charities and the Advertising Council, 1997, pp. 1-13.

32. Bradley cited in Males, *Framing Youth*, p. 341.

33. Jenkins, "Introduction: Childhood Innocence and Other Myths," p. 23.

34. James R. Kincaid, *Child-Loving: The Erotic Child and Victorian Culture* (New York: Routledge, 1992).

35. Higonnet, *Pictures of Innocence*, p. 153.

36. For an excellent analysis of corporate culture and its role in American society, see Charles Derber, *Corporation Nation* (New York: St. Martin's Press, 1998).

37. I am drawing here on the excellent commentary on the sexualization of youth in Higonnet, *Pictures of Innocence*, pp. 154-155.

38. Jenkins, "Introduction: Childhood Innocence and Other Myths," p. 30.

39. For an excellent commentary on how adults construct a number of myths to suggest kids need to be contained for emulating the worst behaviors of adults, see Mike Males, *Framing Youth*. Also, see Ann Powers' insightful commentary on the various ways in which young people defy such stereotypes and make an enormous number of diverse contributions to society, exhibiting both their own sense of individual and collective agency and social contributions to the larger world. I am referring here to Ann Powers, "Who Are These People, Anyway?" *New York Times*, April 29, 1998, pp. 1, 8. For a complex rendering of youth that completely undermines many of the stereotypes circulated about youth, see an adult world punish kids for allegedly imitating the adult behavior emulating the violence, see Jenkins, "Introduction: Childhood Innocence and Other Myths," pp. 1-37. For an excellent collection on the history of youth cultures, see Joe Austin and Michael Nevin Willard, eds., *Generations of Youth* (New York: New York University Press, 1998).

40. Barbara Kantrowitz and Pat Wingert, "How Well Do You Know Your Kid?" *Newsweek*, May 10, 1998, p. 39.

41. I have addressed this issue extensively in Giroux, *Fugitive Cultures;* and Giroux, *Channel Surfing*.

42. Males, *Framing Youth*, pp. 8-9.

43. Cited in Powers, "Who Are These People, Anyway?" p. 8.

44. One index measuring the quality of children's lives claims that the social health of children is at its lowest point in twenty-five years. See *1996 Index of Social Health* (New York: Fordham Institute for Innovation in Social Policy, 1996), p. 6. See also Sylvia Ann Hewlett and Cornel West, *The War Against Parents* (New York: Houghton Mifflin, 1998).

45. Henry A. Giroux, *Border Crossings* (New York: Routledge, 1992) and Henry A. Giroux, *Pedagogy and the Politics of Hope* (Boulder: Westview Press, 1997).

46. Giroux, *Border Crossings*.

47. George Lipsitz, "Listening to Learn and Learning to Listen: Popular Culture, Cultural Theory, and American Studies," *American Quarterly* 42:4 (December 1990), p. 621.

48. I am arguing in this case against those educators who focus on questions of difference almost entirely in terms of identity and subjectivity while ignoring the

related issues of materialism and power. See Henry A. Giroux, *Impure Acts: The Practical Politics of Cultural Studies* (New York: Routledge: forthcoming).

49. Richard Johnson, "Reinventing Cultural Studies: Remembering for the Best Version," in Elizabeth Long, ed., *From Sociology to Cultural Studies* (Malden, Mass: Basil Blackwell, 1997), p. 465.

50. Tony Bennett, "Cultural Studies: A Reluctant Discipline," *Cultural Studies* 12:4 (1998), p. 538.

51. Powers, "Who Are These People, Anyway?"

52. Ibid.

53. Jon Katz, *Virtuous Reality* (New York: Random House, 1997), p. 173.

54. Jenkins, "Testimony Before the U. S. Senate Commerce Committee."

55. Cornel West, "America's Three-Fold Crisis," *Tikkun* 9:2 (1994), pp. 41-42.

56. Grossberg , "Cultural Studies: What's in a Name?" pp. 252-253.

57. West, "America's Three-Fold Crisis," p. 42.

58. Cindy Patton, "Performativity and Spatial Distinction," in Eve Kosofsky Sedgwick and Andrew Parker, eds., *Performativity and Performance* (New York: Routledge, 1993), p. 183.

CHAPTER ONE

1. Marina Warner, *Six Myths of Our Time* (New York: Vintage, 1995), esp. chap. 30. Of course, the concept of childhood innocence as a historical invention has been pointed out by a number of theorists. See, for example, Philip Aries, *Centuries of Childhood* (Harmondsworth: Penguin, 1979); Lloyd deMause, ed., *The Evolution of Childhood* (New York: Psychohistory Press, 1974).

2. Neil Postman, *The Disappearance of Childhood* (New York: Vintage, 1994).

3. See ibid., esp. chap. 8. The notion that television and popular culture represent the main threat to childhood innocence is central to the conservative call for censorship, limiting sex education in the schools, restricting AIDS education, redefining the home as the most important source of moral education, and the "Gumping" of American history (in which the 1960s often are seen as the source of the country's current social ills). The quintessential expression of this position can be found in the speeches, press releases, and writings of former secretary of education and "drug czar" William Bennett. It also can be found in legislation supported by groups such as the Christian Coalition, especially the Parental Rights and Responsibilities Act of 1995. Examples of the conservative position on child abuse, the loss of innocence, and the "poisonous" effects of popular culture abound in the popular press. See, for example, Jeff Stryker, "The Age of Innocence Isn't What It Once Was," *New York Times,* July 13, 1997, p. E3.

4. Cited in Peter Edelman, "The Worst Thing Bill Clinton Has Done," *The Atlantic Monthly* 279 (March 1997), p. 45.

5. All of these figures are taken from two articles on the Children's Defense Fund web site (www.childrensdefense.org/): "The New Welfare Law: One Year Later," October 14, 1997, pp. 1-5, and "CDF, New Studies Look at Status of Former Welfare Recipients," May 27, 1998, pp. 1-4. See also Jennifer Wolch, "American's New Urban Policy: Welfare Reform and the Fate of American Cities," *Journal of American Planning Association* 54:N1 (Winter 1998), pp. 8-11.

6. For specific statistics on the state of youth in the United States, see Children's Defense Fund, *The State of America's Children Yearbook 1998* (Boston: Beacon Press, 1998); Ruth Sidel, *Keeping Women and Children Last* (New York: Penguin, 1996).

7. For an analysis of the ideological underpinnings of the right-wing family values crusade, see Judith Stacey, *In the Name of the Family: Rethinking Family Values in the Postmodern Age* (Boston: Beacon Press, 1996).

8. For an analysis of the widespread assault currently being waged against children, see: Henry A. Giroux, *Channel Surfing: Race Talk and the Destruction of Today's Youth* (New York: St. Martin's Press, 1997); Mike A. Males, *The Scapegoat Generation: America's War on Adolescents* (Monroe, Me.: Common Courage Press, 1996); Charles R. Acland, *Youth, Murder, Spectacle: The Cultural Politics of "Youth in Crisis"* (Boulder, Colo.: Westview Press, 1995); Holly Sklar, "Young and Guilty by Stereotype," *Z Magazine* (July-August 1993): 52-61; Deena Weinstein, "Expendable Youth: The Rise and Fall of Youth Culture," in Jonathan S. Epstein, ed., *Adolescents and Their Music* (New York: Garland, 1994), pp. 67-83; and various articles in *Microphone Fiends*, ed. Andrew Ross and Tricia Rose (New York: Routledge, 1994); Lawrence Grossberg, *We Gotta Get Outta Here* (New York: Routledge, 1992).

9. For a brilliant analysis of how the image of the sexual predator is used to preclude from public discussion the wide range of social factors at work in causing child abuse, see James R. Kincaid, *Child-Loving: The Erotic Child and Victorian Culture* (New York: Routledge, 1992).

10. For an analysis of the Supreme Court's decision, see Linda Greenhouse, "Likely Repeaters May Stay Confined," *New York Times*, June 24, p. A19.

11. The concept of the hollow state comes from Stanley Aronowitz, *The Death and Birth of American Radicalism* (New York: Routledge, 1996).

12. The literature on advertising and the marketing of children's desires is too extensive to cite, but one of the best examples is Stephen Kline, *Out of the Garden: Toys, TV, and Children's Culture in the Age of Marketing* (London: Verso Press, 1993).

13. Richard Goldstein, "The Girl in the Fun Bubble: The Mystery of JonBenet," *Village Voice*, June 10, 1997, p. 41.

14. For a sustained treatment of the current assault on kids, especially those who are poor, nonwhite, and urban, see Henry A. Giroux, *Fugitive Cultures* (New York. Routledge, 1996). See also Angela McRobbie, *Postmodernism and Popular Culture* (New York: Routledge, 1994).

15. Annie Gottlieb, "First Person Sexual," *The Nation*, June 9, 1997, p. 26.

16. Frank Rich, "Let Me Entertain You," *New York Times*, January 18, 1997, Section 1, 23.

17. Goldstein, "The Girl in the Fun Bubble," p. 41.

18. Cited in Karen de Witt, "All Dolled Up," *New York Times*, January 12, 1997, p. D4.

19. While the statistics on children's beauty pageants vary, a number of sources cite similar figures to the ones I cite here. See, for example, Rich, "Let Me Entertain You"; Ellen Mark, "Pretty Babies," *Vogue* (June 1997), p. 240; Beverly Stoeltje, "The Snake Charmer Queen Ritual Competition, and Signification in American Festival," in Colleen Ballerino, Richard Wilk, and Beverly Stoeltje, eds., *Beauty Queens* (New York: Routledge, 1996), p. 13.

20. Cited in Pat Jordan, "The Curious Childhood of an Eleven-Year-Old," *Life* (April 1994), p. 38.

21. In the wake of JonBenet's death, a sharp decline in the popularity of child beauty pageants has resulted in a rise in entry fees. Fees that were once $200 are now $500, thus weeding out all but the most wealthy contestants. See Alex Kuczynski, "Tough Times on the Children's Pageant Circuit," *New York Times*, September 13, 1998, Section 9, p. 1, 8.

22. Mark, "Pretty Babies," p. 240.

23. Linda Caillouet echoes a point made by many academics and journalists across the country: "Pageants have changed over the past 30 years. Grade-schoolers are wearing makeup, modeling swim wear and sashaying down runways. Today's little girls' parents often invest big money in coaches to teach the children the pro-am modeling style and tornado spins. They pay for makeup artists and hair stylists to accompany the children to pageants. Some of the kids use tanning beds. Seven-year-olds have reportedly worn false teeth, false eyelashes, and colored contact lenses." Cited in Linda Caillouet, "Slaying Has Child Pageants on Defensive," Arkansas Democrat-Gazette, April 14, 1997, p. 1A.

24. Jordan, "Curious Childhood," pp. 62, 68.

25. Michael F. Jacobson and Laurie Ann Mazur, Marketing Madness (Boulder, Colo.: Westview, 1995), p. 79.

26. Cited in ad for "Debbrah's: Nation's Top Pageant Designers," Pageant Life (Winter 1996), p. 26.

27. Elliot Zaren, "Eyebrows Lift at Child Strutting in Sexy Dresses, Makeup," Tampa Tribune, January 14, 1997, p. 4.

28. Cited in Jodi Duckett, "In the Eyes of the Beholder: Child Beauty Pageants Get Mixed Reviews," Morning Call, April 6, 1997, p. E1.

29. Ibid.

30. Mark, "Pretty Babies," p. 283.

31. Susan Bordo, Unbearable Weight: Feminism, Western Culture, and the Body (Berkeley: University of California Press, 1993), p. 162.

32. Ibid., p. 179.

33. Naomi Wolf, The Beauty Myth (New York: Anchor Books, 1992).

34. Richard Goldstein, "Nymph Mania: Honoring Innocence in the Breach," Village Voice, June 17, 1997, p. 71. This is not to suggest that women and children do not mediate and resist such domination as much as to make clear the determinate relations of power that lie behind the resurrection of the nymphet in the culture.

35. Stoeltje, "The Snake Charmer," p. 23.

36. Cited in Caillouet, "Slaying Has Child Pageants on Defensive," p. 1A.

37. Cited in Duckett, "In the Eyes," p. E1.

38. See, for example, Susan Faludi, Backlash: The Undeclared War Against American Women (New York: Anchor Books, 1991).

39. This paragraph relies heavily on comments by pediatric psychologists cited in Rebecca A. Eder, Ann Digirolamo, and Suzanne Thompson, "Is Winning a Pageant Worth a Lost Childhood?" St. Louis Post-Dispatch, February 24, 1997, p. 7B.

40. David Elkind, "The Family in the Postmodern World," National Forum 75 (Summer 1995), pp. 24-28.

41. Marly Harris, "Trophy Kids," Money Magazine (March 1997), p. 102.

42. As Annette Corrigan points out, "Young girls should have the freedom to explore the unlimited possibilities of their humanity and to be valued, as men are, for much more than how they look or their capacity to stimulate desire in the opposite sex." Annette Corrigan, "Fashion, Beauty, and Feminism," Meanjin 51:1 (1992), p. 108.

43. For an academic defense of beauty pageants as simply an acting out of community standards, see Michael T. Marsden, "Two Northwestern Ohio Beauty Pageants: A Study in Middle America's Cultural Rituals," in Ray B. Browne and Michael T. Marsden, eds., The Cultures of Celebration (Bowling Green, Ohio: Bowling Green State University Press, 1994), pp. 171-180. Marsden is so intent in seeing pageants as ritualistic performances that he does not notice how ideological his own commentary is when focusing on some of the most sexist

aspects of the pageant practices. Hence, for Marsden, bathing suit competitions simply prove that "beauty can be art." For a more complex analysis see Robert H. Lavender, "'It's Not a Beauty Pageant!' Hybrid Ideology in Minnesota Community Queen Pageants," in *Beauty Queens,* pp. 31-46. See also Susan Orlean's insipid defense of child beauty pageants as public rituals that offer mothers pride when their daughters win and provide pageant contestants the comfort of a family "in which everyone knows each other and watches out for each other." Susan Orlean, "Beautiful Girls," *The New Yorker,* August 4, 1997, pp. 29-36.

44. Stoeltje, "The Snake Charmer Queen Ritual Competition," p. 13.

45. For an important analysis of the different critical approaches to beauty and the politics of appearance that feminists have taken since the appearance of the first Miss America pageant in 1968, see Corrigan, "Fashion, Beauty, and Feminism," pp. 107-22. What is so interesting about this piece is that nothing is said about child beauty pageants. This is especially relevant since many of the conceptual approaches dealing with the politics of appearance simply do not apply to six-year-olds. For instance, the notion that beauty can be appropriated as an act of resistance and turned against the dominant culture seems a bit far-fetched when talking about children who can barely read.

46. One exception can be found in the collection of essays in Cohen et al., eds., *Beauty Queens.*

47. Valerie Walkerdine, *Daddy's Girl: Young Girls and Popular Culture* (Cambridge, Mass: Harvard University Press, 1997), p. 166.

48. While I have not developed in this chapter the implications such depictions have for women, many feminists have provided some excellent analysis. See especially Bordo, *Unbearable* . For a shameful defense of thinness as an aesthetic in the fashion industry, see Rebecca Johnson, "The Body," *Vogue* (September 1997), pp. 653-658. Johnson goes a long way to legitimate some of the most misogynist aspects of the beauty industry, but really reaches into the bottom of the barrel in claiming resentment is the primary reason that many women criticize the image of waiflike models permeating the media. Claiming that thinness is only an aesthetic and not a morality, Johnson seems to forget that within the dominant invocation of thinness as a standard of beauty is the suggestion that overweight women are slovenly, older women are ugly, and nonwhite women are not as beautiful as the ever-present blond waifs who populate the media.

49. The classic work on this issue is Mary Pipher, *Reviving Ophelia: Saving the Selves of Adolescent Girls* (New York: Ballantine Books, 1994). See also Nicole Peradotto, "Little Women: A New Generation of Girls Growing Up Before Their Time," *Buffalo News,* January 26, 1997, p. 1F.

50. Cohen et al., eds., Introduction, to *Beauty Queens,* 10.

51. For a critical analysis of how young girls are represented in popular culture and what is learned by them, see Walkerdine, *Daddy's Girl;* see also McRobbie, *Postmodernism and Popular Culture.*

52. Lawrence Grossberg, "Toward a Genealogy of the State of Cultural Studies," in Cary Nelson and Dilip Parameshwar Gaonkar, eds., *Disciplinarity and Dissent in Cultural Studies* (New York: Routledge, 1996), p. 143.

53. This suggests that adults not only take responsibility for how children's identities are constructed within oppressive social relations but also that such adults support those youth such as Free Children, a youth group consisting of kids between ten and sixteen years of age who are organizing at the national and international level to "to help children being abused and exploited, but to also empower young people to believe in themselves and to believe that they can play an active role as citizens of this world." Craig Kielburger, "Children Can Be Active Citizens of the World," *Rethinking Schools* (Summer 1997), p. 19.

54. Adorno cited in Geoffrey Hartman, "Public Memory and Its Discontents," *Raritan* 8:4 (Spring 1994), p. 27.
55. Stanley Aronowitz, "A Different Perspective on Inequality," in Henry A. Giroux and Patrick Shannon, eds., *Education and Cultural* (New York: Routledge, 1998), p. 193.

CHAPTER TWO

1. This theme is taken up brilliantly in Michael Sorkin, "See You in Disneyland," in Michael Sorkin, ed., *Variations on a Theme Park* (New York: The Noon Day Press, 1992), pp. 205-232.
2. Jean Baudrillard, *Simulacra and Simulation* (Michigan: University of Michigan Press, 1994), p. 87.
3. For a series of articles on what Mark Crispin Miller writing in *The Nation* calls "The National Entertainment State," see the June 3, 1996, issue of *The Nation*.
4. Baudrillard, *Simulacra and Simulation*, pp. 87-88.
5. I am referring here to the infamous conference of artists and academics at Whiskey Pete's Casino in Stateline, Nevada, that included Baudrillard's debut as a Vegas nightclub act. See M. Corrigan, "Vive Las Vegas," *The Village Voice*, November 19, 1996, p. 13.
6. For an insightful piece on art and commerce, see Luis Camnitzer, "Absolut Relativity," *Third Text*, No. 38 (Spring 1997), pp. 86-91.
7. I take this issue up in detail in Henry A. Giroux, *Disturbing Pleasures* (New York: Routledge, 1994). The term "cartoon utopia" is from Michael Sorkin, *Variations on a Theme Park*, p. 232.
8. Camnitzer, "Absolut Relativity," p. 87.
9. Carol Becker, "The Art of Testimony," *Sculpture* 16:3 (March 1997), p. 28.
10. Richard Sennett, "The Social Body," *Transition* 71 (1997), p. 90.
11. Mike Males points out that "Government surveys of returning troops found 30 to 40 percent used heroin regularly and one-fifth described themselves as 'addicted.'" Cited in Mike Males, *Framing Youth* (Monroe, Me.: Common Courage Press, 1999), p. 127.
12. For a personal narrative of heroin use among trendy intellectuals, see Ann M. "Listening to Heroin," *The Village Voice*, April 23, 1994, pp. 25-30; Mark Ehrman, "Heroin Chic," *Playboy* 42:5 (May 1995), pp. 66-68, 144-147.
13. For example, in Seattle between 1986 and 1994 heroin fatalities, primarily among young people, increased by nearly 300 percent. For an analysis of the heroin drug scene in Seattle, see David Lipsky, "Junkie Town," *Rolling Stone*, May 30, 1996, pp. 35-62.
14. The ad appears in *Details* (March 1999), pp. 32-33.
15. I take up this issue in Henry A. Giroux, *Fugitive Cultures: Race, Violence, and Youth* (New York: Routledge, 1996).
16. Ann Powers, "The Hunger," *The Village Voice*, August 23, 1994, p. 29.
17. Cited in Pamela Reynolds, "A Fashion World Hooked on 'Heroin Chic,'" *Boston Globe*, July 26, 1996, p. C1.
18. Clinton cited in Robert A. Rankin, "Clinton Rebukes Fashion Industry for 'Glorification' of Drug Addiction," *Centre Daily Times*, May 21, 1997, p. 6A.
19. Amy M. Spindler argues that "in the last three years some version of the look has been seen in almost every fashion magazine." See Amy M. Spindler, "A Death Tarnishes Fashion's 'Heroin Look,'" *New York Times*, May 20, 1997, p. A25.
20. Both Kuramoto and Kemp cited in Warren Richey, "Boycott Groups: Klein Ads Carry Scent of 'Heroin Chic,'" *The Christian Science Monitor*, October 25, 1996, p. 3.

21. Robert Triefus, a senior vice president at Calvin Klein, cited in ibid.
22. Corrine Day's work can be seen in Camilla Nickerson and Neville Wakefield, eds., *Fashion* (Berlin: Scalo, 1996).
23. Day says "I like beauty the way I find it, and I don't want to disturb it." Cited in Holly Brubach, "Beyond Shocking," *New York Times Magazine,* May 18, 1997, p. 26.
24. Reynolds, "A Fashion World Hooked on 'Heroin Chic.'"
25. Both Jones and Nguyen are cited in Richard B. Woodward, "Whither Fashion Photography," *New York Times,* June 8, 1997, p. 58.
26. Laura Craik, "Heroin Chic? Just Say No," *The Guardian,* May 23, 1997, p. 19.
27. See Richard Harvey Brown, "Realism and Power in Aesthetic Representation," in Richard Brown, ed., *Postmodern Representations* (Bloomington: Indiana University Press, 1995), pp. 134-167.
28. Ibid., p. 135.
29. I am drawing in this case on the work of Zygmunt Bauman, *Life in Fragments* (Cambridge: Basil Blackwell, 1995), especially "Violence and Postmodernism," pp. 139-162.
30. Geoffrey Hartman, "Public Memory and Its Discontents," *Raritan* 8:4 (Spring 1994), p. 28.

CHAPTER THREE

1. John Dewey, *Democracy and Education* (New York: Free Press, 1916); Henry Giroux, *Schooling and the Struggle for Public Life* (Minneapolis: University of Minnesota Press, 1988); David Sehr, *Education for Democracy* (Albany: State University of New York Press, 1996).
2. Michael Jacobson and Laurie Masur, *Laurie Marketing Madness* (Boulder, Colo.: Westview, 1995); Alex Molnar, *Giving Kids the Business* (Boulder, Colo.: Westview, 1996); Consumer Union Education Service, *Captive Kids: A Report on Commercial Pressures on Kids at School* (Yonkers, N.Y. Consumer Union Education Services, 1998).
3. Cited in Stanley Aronowitz, "The New Corporate University," *Dollars and Sense* (March/April 1998), p. 3
4. All quotes cited in Randall C. Archibold, "Applying Corporate Touch to a Troubled School District," *The New York Times* (Tuesday, October 12, 1999), p. A28.
5. Cited in Peter Applebome, "Lure of the Education Market Remains Strong for Business," *New York Times,* January 31, 1996, p. A1.
6. Cited in Russell Baker, "The Education of Mike Milken: From Junk-Bond King to Master of the Knowledge Universe," *The Nation,* May 3, 1999, p. 12.
7. See Russell Baker's commentary on Milken's launching of Knowledge Universe, with revenues of $1.2 billion, and an insatiable reach for buying everything that appears to have any potential for making a profit in the educational marketplace. In ibid., pp. 11-18.
8. Phyllis Vine, "To Market, to Market," *The Nation,* September 8-15, 1997, pp. 11-17.
9. David W. Kirkpatrick, *Choice in Schooling: A Case for Tuition Vouchers* (Chicago: Loyala University Press, 1990); Diane Ravitch, *Debating the Future of American Education* (Washington, D.C.: Brookings Institute, 1995). Many of these reports are produced by right-wing think tanks with a vested interest in the privatization movement. For example, see Paul Pekin, "Schoolhouse Crock: Right-Wing Myths Behind the 'New Stupidity,'" *Extra!* (January/February 1998), pp. 9-10. For an excellent rebuttal of the charge that American public education is in a state of disastrous decline, see David Berliner and Bruce Biddle, *The Manufactured Crisis* (Reading, Mass.: Addison Wesley, 1995); Gerald Bracey, "What

Happened to America's Public Schools? Not What You Think?" *American Heritage* (November 1997), pp. 39-52.

10. Cited in Vine, "To Market, to Market," p. 12.

11. Cited in ibid., p. 11.

12. For a summary of the historical failures of privatization, see the Carol Ascher, Norm Fruchter, and Robert Berne, *Hard Lessons: Public Schools and Privatization* (New York: The Twentieth Century Fund, 1996). For a specific analysis of the failure of Education Alternatives, Inc., in Baltimore and Hartford, see Molnar, *Giving Kids the Business,* esp. chap. 4, pp. 77-116. Also, see Vine, "To Market, To Market," pp. 11-17; Bruce Shapiro, "Privateers Flunk Schools," *The Nation,* February 19, 1998, p. 4.

13. Jonathan Kozol, "Saving Public Education," *The Nation,* February 17, 1997, p. 16.

14. Richard J. Herrnstein and Charles Murray, *The Bell Curve* (New York: The Free Press, 1994).

15. This is particularly true as schools engage in market-sponsored contests in which teachers spend valuable teaching time coaching kids how to collect cash receipts, sell goods to their friends and neighbors, or learn the rules for bring in profits for companies who then offer prizes to schools. See Molnar, *Giving Kids the Business,* esp. chap. 3.

16. David Labaree, "Are Students 'Consumers'?" , September 17, 1997, p. 48.

17. Kathleen Kennedy Manzo, "California School Board Infusing Pedagogy Into Frameworks," *Education Week,* March 11, 1998, p. 7.

18. Deborah W. Meier, "Saving Public Education," *The Nation,* February 17, 1997, p. 24.

19. Alan O'Shea, "A Special Relationship? Academia and Pedagogy," *Cultural Studies* 12:4 (1998), pp. 521-522.

20. Stanley Aronowitz, "Introduction," in Paulo Freire, *Pedagogy of Freedom: Ethics, Democracy, and Civic Courage* (Lanham, Md.: Rowman and Littlefield, 1998), pp. 4-5.

21. Svi Shapiro, "Public School Reform: The Mismeasure of Education," *Tikkun* 13:1 (Winter 1998), p. 54. See also Henry A. Giroux, *Teachers as Intellectuals* (Westport, Conn.: Bergin and Garvey Press, 1988); Stanley Aronowitz and Henry A. Giroux, *Education Still Under Siege* (Westport, Conn.: Bergin and Garvey Press, 1993).

22. Baker, "Education of Mike Milken," p. 17.

23. I take up this issue in Henry A. Giroux, *The Mouse That Roared: Disney and the End of Innocence* (Lanham, Md.: Rowman and Littlefield, 1999).

24. Russell Mokhiber and Robert Weissman, *Corporate Predators* (Monroe, Me.: Common Courage Press, 1999), p. 168.

25. Jeffrey Henig, "The Danger of Market Rhetoric," in Robert Lowe and Barbara Miner, eds., *Selling Out Our Schools* (Milwaukee: Rethinking Schools Institute, 1996), p. 11. See also Jeffrey Henig, *Rethinking School Choice* (Princeton, N.J.: Princeton University Press, 1994).

26. Consumer Union, *Captive.*

27. Phyllis Sides, "Captive Kids: Teaching Students to be Consumers," in *Selling Out Our Schools: Vouchers, Markets, and the Future of Public Education* (Milwaukee: Rethinking Schools Publication, 1996), p. 36.

28. For an extensive analysis of Channel One, see Henry A. Giroux, *Disturbing Pleasures: Learning Popular Culture* (New York: Routledge, 1994), esp. chap. 3, "pp. 47-67.

29. Steven Manning, "Classrooms for Sale," *New York Times,* March 4, 1999, p. A27; see also, Steven Manning "Zapped," *The Nation,* September 27, 1999, p. 9.

30. Cover story, "This Lesson Is Brought to You By," *Business Week,* June 30, 1997, p. 69.

31. Ibid.
32. Cited in Editors, "Reading, Writing . . . and Purchasing," *Educational Leadership* 56:2 (1998), p. 16.
33. Manning, "Classrooms for Sale," p. A27.
34. For a brilliant analysis of how citizenship is being privatized within an expanding corporate culture, see Lauren Berlant, *The Queen of America Goes to Washington* (Durham, N.C.: Duke University Press, 1997).
35. Consumer Union, *Captive Kids,* p. 9.
36. Ibid., p. 26.
37. Mary B. W. Tabor, "Schools Profit From Offering Pupils for Market Research," *New York Times,* April 5, 1999, pp. A1, A16.
38. Ibid., p. A16.
39. Cited in Steven Manning, "How Corporations Are Buying Their Way into America's Classroom," *The Nation* (September 27, 1999), p. 12.
40. Tabor, "Schools Profit From Offering Pupils for Market Research," p. A16.
41. This issue is taken up in great detail in Molnar, *Giving Kids the Business.* For a more general analysis of the relationship between corporate culture and schooling, see Joe Kincheloe and Shirley Steinberg, eds., *KinderCulture: The Corporate Construction of Childhood* (Boulder, Colo.: Westview, 1997).
42. Gerald Grace, "Politics, Markets, and Democratic Schools: On the Transformation of School Leadership," in A. H. Halsey, Hugh Lauder, Phillip Brown, and Amy Stuart Wells, eds., *Education: Culture, Economy, Society* (New York: Oxford, 1997), p. 314.
43. Ibid., p. 315.
44. R. George Wright, *Selling Words: Free Speech in a Commercial Culture* (New York: New York University Press, 1997), p. 181.
45. Ibid., p. 182.
46. David Stratman, "School Reform and the Attack on Public Education," *Dollars and Sense* (March/April 1988), p. 7.
47. Nor am I suggesting that corporations cannot play a fundamental role in expanding democratic values. See, for example, the role of groups such as Business Leaders for Sensible Priorities, that have lobbied to decrease military spending in favor of investing in public resources such as schools, health care, and the like. See the powerful ad placed by the group against increases in military spending in *New York Times,* March 24, 1999, p. A21.
48. Dewey, *Democracy and Education.*
49. Molnar, *Giving Kids the Business,* p. 17.
50. This issue is explored in Ken Saltman, "Collateral Damage: Public School Privatization and the Threat to Democracy," Ph.D. Diss., Pennsylvania State University, May 1999, p. 92.
51. A number of books take up the relationship between schooling and democracy; some of the more important recent critical contributions include: Elizabeth A. Kelly, *Education, Democracy, & Public Knowledge* (Boulder, Colo.: Westview, 1995); Wilfred Carr and Anthony Hartnett, *Education and the Struggle for Democracy* (Philadelphia: Open University Press, 1996); Sehr, *Education for Public Democracy;* James Fraser, *Reading, Writing and Justice: School Reform as If Democracy Matters* (Albany: State University of New York Press, 1997); see also Giroux, *Schooling and the Struggle for Public Life;* and Henry A. Giroux, *Pedagogy and the Politics of Hope* (Boulder, Colo.: Westview, 1997).
52. Robin D. G. Kelley, "Neo-Cons of the Black Nation," *Black Renaissance Noire* 1:2 (Summer/Fall 1997), p. 146.
53. Ascher, Fruchter, and Berne, *Hard Lessons,* p. 112.
54. Manning, "Classrooms for Sale," p. A27.

55. Cornel West, "America's Three-Fold Crisis," *Tikkun* 9:2 (1994), p. 42.
56. See Steven Manning, "How Corporations Are Buying Their Way Into Classrooms," op. cit., p. 15
57. "Short Subjects," *Chronicle of Higher Education*, March 13, 1998, p. A11.

CHAPTER FOUR

I would like to thank Nick Burbules for his editorial help on this chapter.

1. For example, see Todd Gitlin, *The Twilight of Common Dreams* (New York: Metropolitan Books, 1995); Richard Rorty, "The Dark Side of the Academic Left," *Chronicle of Higher Education,* April 3, 1998, pp. B4-B6.
2. For a critique of the tendency of theorists such as Todd Gitlin to pit class politics against identity and cultural politics, see Robin D. G. Kelley, *Yo' Mama's Disfunktional: Fighting the Culture Wars in Urban America* (Boston: Beacon Press, 1998), esp. chap. 4, "Looking Extremely Backward: Why the Enlightenment Will Only Lead Us into the Dark," pp. 102-124. Also, see Henry A. Giroux, *Impure Acts: The Practical Politics of Cultural Studies,* New York: Routledge, forthcoming.
3. John Frow and Meghan Morris cited in Lawrence Grossberg, *Bringing It All Back Home: Essays on Cultural Studies* (Durham, N.C.: Duke University Press, 1977), p. 268.
4. Terry Cochran, "Culture in Its Sociohistorical Dimension," *Boundary* 21:2 (1994), p. 157.
5. Lawrence Grossberg, "Toward a Genealogy of the State of Cultural Studies," in Cary Nelson and Dilip Parameshwar Gaonkar, eds., *Disciplinarity and Dissent in Cultural Studies* (New York: Routledge, 1996), p. 142.
6. See, for example, Herbert I. Schiller, *Culture Inc.: The Corporate Takeover of Public Expression* (New York: Oxford University Press, 1989); Erik Barnouw, ed., *Conglomerates and the Media* (New York: Free Press, 1997). Edward S. Herman and Robert W. Chesney, *The Global Media,* (Washington: Cassell, 1997); Robert W. McChesney, *Rich Media, Poor Democracy* (Urbana: University of Illinois Press, 1999).
7. Henry A. Giroux, "Talking Heads: Public Intellectuals and Radio Pedagogy," *Art Papers* (July/August 1995), pp. 17-21.
8. Antonio Gramsci, *Selections from the Prison Notebooks,* trans. and ed. by Quintin Hoare and Geoffrey Nowell Smith (New York: International Publishers, 1971), p. 350.
9. Children's Defense Fund, *State of America's Children Yearbook 1998* (Boston: Beacon Press, 1998). More specifically, "In 1995, 14.7 million children (21 percent of America's children) were living in poverty, 2.1 million more than in 1989)" (p. 17).
10. This issue is taken up in Stanley Aronowitz, *The Death and Rebirth of American Radicalism* (New York: Routledge, 1996).
11. On this issue, see Michael Tonry, *Malign Neglect: Race, Crime, and Punishment in America* (New York: Oxford University Press, 1995); James G. Miller, *Search and Destroy: African-American Males in the Criminal Justice System* (New York: Cambridge University Press, 1996); Fox Butterfield, "Crime Keeps on Falling, But Prisons Keep on Filling," *New York Times,* September 28, 1997, Section 4, p. 1. David Cole, *No Equal Justice: Race and Class in the American Criminal Justice System* (New York: The New Press, 1999).
12. In this case, I am referring specifically to the widely popularized work of Charles Murray and Richard J. Herrnstein: *The Bell Curve* (New York: Free Press, 1994). For three important critical responses to Murray and Herrnstein, see Russell Jacoby and Naomi Glauberman, eds., *The Bell Curve Debate* (New York: Random

House, 1995); Joe L. Kincheloe, Shirley Steinberg, and Aaron D. Gresson III, eds., *Measured Lies: The Bell Curve Examined* (New York: St. Martin's Press, 1996); Claude Fisher, Michael Hout, Martin Sanchez Jankowski, Samuel Lucas, Ann Swidler, and Kim Voss, *Inequality by Design: Cracking the Bell Curve Myth* (Princeton, N.J.: Princeton University Press, 1996).

13. See, for example, Kofi Buenor Hadjor, *Another America: The Politics of Race and Blame* (Boston: South End Press, 1995); Andrew Hacker, *Two Nations: Black and White, Separate, Hostile, and Unequal*(New York: Scribner, 1995); Manning Marable, *Beyond Black and White* (London: Verso, 1995); David K. Shipler, *A Country of Strangers* (New York: Vintage, 1998).

14. For some excellent recent sources on the corporatization of the university, see Evan Watkins, *Work Time: English Departments and the Circulation of Cultural Value* (Stanford, Calif.: Stanford University Press, 1989); Stanley Aronowitz and William DiFazio, *The Jobless Future* (Minneapolis: University of Minnesota Press, 1994), esp. chap. 8, pp. 226-263. Cary Nelson, ed., *Will Teach for Food: Academic Labor in Crisis* (Minneapolis: University of Minnesota Press, 1997); Randy Martin, ed. *Chalk Lines: The Politics of Work in the Managed University* (Durham: Duke University Press, 1998).

15. See, for example, Bill Readings, *The University in Ruins* (Cambridge: Harvard University Press, 1996); Stanley Aronowitz, *The Knowledge Factory* (Boston: Beacon Press, 2000).

16. The notion of thinking in Gramscian terms comes from Paul Bove, "Foreword," in Marcia Landy, *Film, Politics, and Gramsci* (Minneapolis: University of Minnesota Press, 1994), p. xvi.

17. Raymond Williams, *Communications* (New York: Barnes & Noble, 1967), p. 15.

18. Joseph Buttigieg is on target in arguing that while Gramsci's writings are fragmentary, there is nothing unclear about his views regarding "the relation between the theoretical work of intellectuals and political praxis." See Joseph Buttigieg, "After Gramsci," *Midwestern Modern Language Association* 24:1 (Spring 1991), p. 93.

19. Harold Entwistle, *Antonio Gramsci: Conservative Schooling for Radical Politics* (Boston: Routledge and Kegan Paul, 1989); E. D. Hirsch, Jr., *The Schools We Need* (New York: Doubleday, 1996).

20. Hirsch misrepresents the work of critical theorists in education a number of times in his book. For instance, he completely misreads the work of the French sociologist Pierre Bourdieu by claiming that his analysis of "cultural capital" is important because it provides the basis for working-class children to succeed in schools. Of course, cultural capital for Bourdieu was a class-specific category based on the Marxist notion of exchange value and used to illuminate how middle-class cultural capital is used in schools to legitimate forms of class inequality. See Walter Feinberg's analysis of Hirsch's distortion of Bourdieu's work in "Educational Manifestos and the New Fundamentalism," *Educational Researcher* 26:8 (November 1997), pp. 27-35.

21. My analysis of Entwistle draws from an early review in Henry A. Giroux, "Essay Review of Antonio Gramsci: Conservative Schooling for Radical Politics by Harold Entwistle," *Telos* 45 (Fall 1980), pp. 215-225.

22. Entwistle, *Gramsci*, p. 177.

23. Douglas Holly, "Antonio Gramsci: Conservative Schooling for Radical Politics," *British Journal of the Sociology of Education* 1:3 (1980), p. 319.

24. Hirsch, *Schools We Need*, p. 7.

25. David Forgacs, "Working-Class Education and Culture: Introduction," in David Forgacs, ed., *An Antonio Gramsci Reader* (New York: Schocken, 1988), p. 54.

26. Antonio Gramsci, "Socialism and Culture," in Paul Piccone and Pedro Caval-cante, eds., *History, Philosophy, and Culture in the Young Gramsci* (St. Louis: Telos Press, 1975), pp. 20-21.
27. Hirsch, *Schools We Need*, p. 113.
28. Ibid.
29. Gramsci, *Selections from the Prison Notebooks*, p. 30.
30. Ibid., pp. 32-33.
31. Jerome Karabel, "Revolutionary Contradictions: Antonio Gramsci and the Problem of Intellectuals," *Politics and Society* 6 (1976), p. 172.
32. Gramsci, *Selections from the Prison Notebooks*, p. 42.
33. Ibid.
34. Gramsci, "Men or Machines," p. 62.
35. Ibid., p. 64.
36. Hirsch, *Schools We Need*, p. 7.
37. Ibid.
38. For an analysis of schools within a broader political, cultural, and economic context, see Henry A. Giroux, *Pedagogy and the Politics of Hope* (Boulder, Colo.: Westview, 1997).
39. Gramsci, *Selections from the Prison Notebooks*, p. 350.
40. Gramsci cited in Edward Said, *The World, the Text, and the Critic* (Cambridge, Mass.: Harvard University Press, 1983), p. 172.
41. For in-depth analyses of the work of E. D. Hirsch, see Stanley Aronowitz and Henry A. Giroux, "Schooling, Culture, and Literacy in the Age of Broken Dreams: A Review of Bloom and Hirsch," *Harvard Educational Review* 58:2 (May 1988), pp. 171-194; Barbara Hernstein Smith, "Cult-Lit: Hirsch, Literacy and the National Culture," *South Atlantic Quarterly* 89:1 (Winter 1990), pp. 69-88; Walter Feinberg, "Educational Manifestos and the New Fundamentalism," *Educational Researcher* 26:8 (November 1997), pp. 27-35; Kristen L. Burns, "Questioning Core Assumptions: A Critical Reading of and Response to E. P. Hirsch's *The Schools We Need and Why We Don't Have Them*," *Harvard Educational Review* 69:1 (1999), pp. 67-93.
42. Nancy Fraser, "From Redistribution to Recognition? Dilemmas of Justice in a 'Post-Socialist' Age," *New Left Review* 212 (July/August 1995), p. 71.
43. Stuart Hall, "Subjects in History: Making Diasporic Identities," in Wahneema Lubiano, ed., *The House that Race Built* (New York: Pantheon, 1997), p. 297.
44. Hirsch, *Schools We Need*, pp. 103-104.
45. Chandra Talpade Mohanty, "On Race and Voice: Challenge for Liberal Education in the 1990s," *Cultural Critique*, No. 14 (Winter 1989-1990), p. 184.
46. Said, *The World, the Text, and the Critic*, p. 169.
47. Mohanty, "On Race and Voice," p. 192.
48. Landy, *Film, Politics, and Gramsci*, p. 26.
49. Gramsci cited in Cochran, "Culture in Its Sociohistorical Dimension," p. 153.
50. On Gramsci's contribution to this issue, see Said, *The World, the Text, and the Critic*, p. 171.
51. Paul Berman, "The Philosopher-King Is Mortal," *New York Times Magazine*, May 11, 1997, p. 37.

CHAPTER FIVE

1. My reference to the public sphere draws primarily from the following: Jurgen Habermas, *The Structural Transformation of the Public Sphere*, trans. Thomas Burger (Cambridge, Mass.: MIT Press, 1989); various papers collected in Craig Calhoun, ed., *Habermas and the Public Sphere* (Cambridge, Mass.: MIT Press,

1992), especially Nancy Fraser, "Rethinking the Public Sphere: A Contribution to the Critique of Actually Existing Democracy," pp. 99-108; Oscar Negt and Alexander Kluge, *Public Sphere and Experience: Toward an Analysis of the Bourgeois and Proletarian Public Sphere* (Minneapolis: University of Minnesota Press, 1993); Chantal Mouffe, *The Return of the Political* (London: Verso, 1993); Bruce Robbins, ed., *The Phantom Public Sphere* (Minneapolis: University of Minnesota Press, 1993).

2. Stanley Aronowitz, "The Situation of the Left in the United States," *Socialist Review* 23:3 (1994), p. 59.

3. Sarah Pollock, "Robert Haas," *Mother Jones* (March/April 1997), p. 22.

4. My notion of the oppositional or counter-public sphere is developed in Negt and Kluge, *Public Sphere and Experience*. See also Henry A. Giroux, *Border Crossings: Cultural Workers and the Politics of Education* (New York: Routledge, 1992), and Stanley Aronowitz and Henry A. Giroux, *Education Still Under Siege* (Westport, Conn.: Bergin and Garvey, 1993).

5. A classic example of this type of critique can be found in Illan Gur-Ze'ev, "Toward a Nonrepresentative Critical Pedagogy," *Educational Theory* 48:4 (Fall 1998), pp. 463-486. This piece suggests that Freire shares a dogmatic idealism that puts his work in the same camp as national socialist ideologues. It also argues that Freire's teaching is noncritical in that it posits the knowledge of the oppressed as self-evident and unproblematic. Such pieces are not only theoretically silly but harbor a mean-spirited cynicism that banishes hope from the very realm of politics.

6. Simon Frith, *Performance Rites* (Cambridge, Mass.: Harvard University Press, 1996), p. 204.

7. Herman Gray, "Is Cultural Studies Inflated?" in Cary Nelson and Dilip Parameshway Goankar, eds., *Disciplinarity and Dissent in Cultural Studies* (New York: Routledge, 1996), p. 211.

8. Cited in Joy James, *Transcending the Talented Tenth: Black Leaders and American Intellectuals* (New York: Routledge, 1997), p. 175.

9. Richard Johnson, "Reinventing Cultural Studies: Remembering for the Best Version," in Elizabeth Long, ed., *From Sociology to Cultural Studies* (Malden, Mass: Basil Blackwell, 1997), p. 464.

10. Marcuse cited in Stanley Aronowitz, "The Unknown Herbert Marcuse," *Social Text* 17:1 (Spring 1999), p. 139.

11. Martha C. Nussbaum, "The Professor of Parody," *The New Republic,* February 22, 1999, p. 42. While I agree with some of the general issues raised in Nussbaum's piece, I think she is completely wrong in her critique of Judith Butler and reduces the latter's position to a caricature.

12. Two typical examples of this discourse, characterized by Martha C. Nussbaum as "hip quietism," can be found in Elizabeth Ellsworth, *Teaching Positions* (New York: Teachers College Press, 1997); Mimi Orner, Janet Miller, and Elizabeth Ellsworth, "Excessive Moments and Educational Discourses that Try to Contain Them," *Educational Theory* 45:4 (Fall 1996), pp. 71-91.

13. Cited in Stanley Aronowitz, "Introduction," in Paulo Freire, *Pedagogy of Freedom* (Lanham, Md.: Rowman and Littlefield, 1998), p. 6.

14. Paulo Freire, *Pedagogy of Hope* (New York: Continuum Press, 1994), pp. 8-9.

15. See especially Paulo Freire, *The Politics of Education* (Westport, Conn.: Bergin and Garvey, 1985); Paulo Freire and Donaldo Macedo, *Literacy: Reading the Word and the World* (Wesport, Conn.: Bergin and Garvey, 1987); See also Henry A. Giroux, "Introduction," in Freire, *Politics of Education,* pp. xi-xxv.

16. For a classic analysis of this position, George Counts, *Dare the School Build a New Social Order* (New York: John Day, 1932); Lawrence Cremin, *The Transformation*

of the School: Progressivism in American Education, 1876-1957 (New York: Random House, 1961). For a more recent critical analysis of this position, see Aronowitz and Giroux, *Education Still Under Siege*; James Fraser, *Reading, Writing, and Justice: School Reform as If Democracy Matters* (Albany, N.Y.: State University of New York Press, 1997).

17. On this issue, see Cremin, *Transformation of the School.*

18. For a succinct commentary on this issue, see David F. Labaree, "Are Students 'Consumers'?" *Education Week,* September 17, 1997, pp. 18-19.

19. For an analysis of schooling as a site of reproduction and resistance, see Giroux, *Theory and Resistance in Education* (Westport, CT: Bergin and Garvey Press, 1983), and Giroux, *Schooling and the Struggle for Democratic Public Life.*

20. A classic statement on this issue can be found in Newt Gingrich, *To Renew America* (New York: HarperCollins, 1995).

21. For an excellent analysis of the right-wing attack on the welfare state, see Stanley Aronowitz, *The Death and Rebirth of American Radicalism* (New York: Routledge, 1996). For an analysis of how this attack particularly affects children, see Ruth Sidel, *Keeping Women and Children Last* (New York: Penguin Books, 1996).

22. I take this issue up in Henry A. Giroux, *Channel Surfing: Race Talk and the Destruction of American Youth* (New York: St. Martin's Press, 1997).

23. Aronowitz, "Introduction," in Freire, *Pedagogy of Freedom,* p. 4.

24. Freire, *Pedagogy of Hope,* p. 91.

25. Ibid., p. 9.

26. Of course, this position is clearly articulated in Freire's early work, such as *Pedagogy of the Oppressed,* trans. Myra Bergman Ramos (New York: Seabury Press, 1973), but can also be found in his later work as well.

27. Stanley Aronowitz, "Paulo Freire's Democratic Humanism," in Peter McLaren and Peter Leonard, eds., *Paulo Freire: A Critical Encounter* (New York: Routledge, 1993), p. 17.

28. One recent example of this can be found in Alice McIntyre, *Making Meaning of Whiteness* (Albany: State University of New York Press, 1997), pp. 19-20. McIntyre refers to Freire's work as a "methodology for learning" as if such a "methodology" can be understood outside of the specific historical context, radical political theory, and specific set of social formations and conditions that produced it. The refusal to contextualize Freire's work betrays a positivist refusal to deal with the relationship between political projects and the emergence of specific educational formations.

29. Paulo Freire, *Letters to Christina: Reflections on My Life and Work* (New York: Routledge, 1996), pp. 113-114.

30. Lawrence Grossberg, *Bringing It All Back Home: Essays on Cultural Studies* (Durham, N.C.: Duke University Press, 1997), p. 264.

31. Ibid., p. 262.

32. Antonio Gramsci, *Selections from the Prison Notebooks,* trans. Q. Hoare and G. Smith (New York: International Press, 1971), p. 350.

33. Homi Bhabha, "The Enchantment of Art," in Carol Becker and Ann Wiens, eds., *The Artists in Society* (Chicago: New Art Examiner, 1994), p. 28.

34. Aronowitz, "Introduction," in Freire, *Pedagogy of Freedom,* pp. 10-11.

35. Freire, *Pedagogy of the Oppressed,* p. 142.

36. Jane Gallop, *Feminist Accused of Sexual Harassment* (Durham, N.C.: Duke University Press, 1997), p. 62. Gallop relates a chilling story about her own colleagues who opposed a conference she was organizing on the grounds that it would make students "unhappy or remind them of painful experiences." Gallop rightly criticizes this position and argues that "We who were planning the conference considered it our primary duty to foster knowledge. Inasmuch as we

were teachers, it was our responsibility to expose students to as much learning as possible. Protecting students from knowledge that would make them uncomfortable seemed ultimately a failure to teach them, placing some other relationship above our duty as their teachers. . . . We . . . assumed that what women most need is knowledge and that women students are tough enough to learn" (pp. 61-62). While this critique is applied to some versions of feminist education, the notion that the educational goal of making students feel good—and conversely not making them uncomfortable in the learning process—has become one of the defining features of a number of strands of critical educational practices. I would argue such a position is the ideological and educational antithesis of what Freire had in mind when he talked about dialogue and sharing power with students.

37.   Lauren Berlant, "Feminism and the Institutions of Intimacy," in E. Ann Kaplan and George Levine, eds., *The Politics of Research* (New York: Routledge, 1997), pp. 153-154.

38.   Freire cited in Freire and Macedo, "A Dialogue," p. 214.

39.   Ibid., p. 202.

40.   Gerald Graff, *Beyond the Culture Wars: How Teaching the Conflicts Can Revitalize American Education* (New York: Norton, 1992). For an insightful rebuttal of Graff's attack on radical pedagogy, see Freire and Macedo, "A Dialogue," pp. 188-228.

41.   Freire and Macedo, "A Dialogue," p. 202.

42.   Freire, cited in ibid.

43.   bell hooks, "Black Students Who Reject Feminism," *Chronicle of Higher Education*, July 13, 1994, p. A44. hooks also provides an excellent feminist analysis of Paulo Freire's educational system in bell hooks, "Bell Hooks Speaking About Paulo Freire—The Man, His Work," in McLaren and Leonard, eds., *Paulo Freire*, pp. 146-154.

44.   Surely Freire would have agreed wholeheartedly with Stuart Hall's insight that: "It is only through the way in which we represent and imagine ourselves that we come to know how we are constituted and who we are. There is no escape from the politics of representation." Stuart Hall, "What Is This 'Black' in Popular Culture?" in Gina Dent, ed., *Black Popular Culture* (Seattle: Bay Press, 1992), p. 30. At the same time, Freire was as much concerned with what educators do with language as with decoding its meanings.

45.   Paulo Freire died of a heart attack on May 2, 1997, in a hospital in São Paulo, Brazil.

CHAPTER SIX

1.   An excellent bibliography of Stuart Hall's work can be found in a collection of his writings compiled by David Morley and Kuan-Hsing Chen: *Stuart Hall: Critical Dialogues in Cultural Studies* (New York: Routledge, 1996).

2.   This is not to suggest that Hall underestimates the importance of deconstructive work with regard to analyzing various cultural texts. On the contrary, arguing against an exclusive focus on textuality, Hall writes:

> The text is abstracted from its institutional context, from its historical context—that form of what I would call "literary cultural studies" is deeply troubling. You have to work on the text, but you also have to work on the context; you have to know something about the history of the society in which the institutions work as well as about what the technologies of the media are and how they're financed. So, I think

there's been a kind of reduction to text in the narrow sense, not text in the broad sense, indicating what I call the discursive turn.

3. Stuart Hall cited in Julie Drew, "Cultural Composition: Stuart Hall on Ethnicity and the Discursive Turn," *Journal of Composition Theory* 18:2 (1998), p. 184.

4. Peter Osborne and Lynne Segal, "Culture and Power: Interview with Stuart Hall," *Radical Philosophy,* No. 86 (November/December 1997), p. 24.

5. Hall elaborates his theory of culture best in a series of books designed for the Culture, Media, and Identities Series at Open University and published by Sage in the United States. See, for example, Stuart Hall, Paul du Gay, Linda Janes, Hugh Mackay, and Keith Negus, *Doing Cultural Studies: The Story of the Sony Walkman* (Thousand Oaks, Calif.: Sage, 1997); Stuart Hall, *Representation: Cultural Representations and Signifying Practices* (Thousand Oaks, Calif.: Sage, 1997); Stuart Hall, "The Centrality of Culture: Notes on the Cultural Revolutions of Our Time," in Kenneth Thompson, ed., *Media and Cultural Regulation* (Thousand Oaks, Calif.: Sage, 1997).

6. For an excellent analysis of Stuart Hall's work, see Lawrence Grossberg, "History, Politics, and Postmodernism: Stuart Hall and Cultural Studies," *Bringing It All Back Home: Essays on Cultural Studies* (Durham, N.C.: Duke University Press, 1997), pp. 174-194. See also Morley and Chen, eds., *Stuart Hall.*

7. Harold Bloom, *The Western Canon* (New York: Riverhead Books, 1994); Richard Rorty, *Achieving Our Country: Leftist Thought in Twentieth Century America* (Cambridge, Mass.: Harvard University Press, 1998); Richard Rorty, "The Inspirational Value of Great Works of Literature," *Raritan* 16:1 (1996), pp. 8-17; Todd Gitlin, *Twilight of Our Common Dreams* (New York: Metropolitan Books, 1995).

8. Lawrence Grossberg, "Identity and Cultural Studies. Is That All There Is?" in Stuart Hall and Paul du Gay, eds., *Questions of Cultural Identity* (Thousand Oaks, Calif.: Sage, 1996), p. 102.

9. Lawrence Grossberg, "Toward a Genealogy of the State of Cultural Studies," in Gary Nelson and Dilip Parameshwar Gaonkar, eds., *Disciplinarity and Dissent in Cultural Studies* (New York: Routledge, 1996), p. 142.

10. Stuart Hall, "Race, Culture, and Communications: Looking Backward and Forward at Cultural Studies," *Rethinking Marxism* 5:1 (Spring 1992), pp. 17-18.

11. I critique the conservative attack on political correctness in Henry A. Giroux, *Fugitive Cultures* (New York: Routledge, 1996), esp. pp. 165-184.

12. Matthew Arnold, "Sweetness and Light," in *The Complete Prose of Matthew Arnold,* Vol. 5, ed. R. H. Super (Ann Arbor: University of Michigan Press, 1960-1977), p. 113.

13. See Gitlin, *Twilight of Our Common Dreams;* Michael Tomasky, *Left for Dead: The Life, Death and Possible Resurrection of Progressive Politics in America* (New York: Free Press, 1996); Jim Sleeper, *The Closest of Strangers* (New York: Norton, 1990).

14. Gitlin's most sustained development of this argument can be found in *Twilight of Our Common Dreams.*

15. Judith Butler, "Merely Cultural," *Social Text* 15:52-53 (Fall/Winter, 1997), p. 266.

16. For an insightful analysis of this position, see Grossberg, "Cultural Studies," pp. 245-271.

17. Todd Gitlin, "The Anti-Political Populism of Cultural Studies," *Dissent* (Spring 1997), p. 81.

18. Ibid., p. 82.

NOTES TO CHAPTER SIX

19. Stuart Hall, "The Emergence of Cultural Studies and the Crisis of the Humanities," *October,* No. 53 (Summer 1990), p. 18.
20. Gitlin, "Anti-Political Populism of Cultural Studies."
21. One particularly important source on cultural studies can be found in Grossberg, *Bringing It All Back Home.* I mention this book because Grossberg's work defies the simplistic analysis given by most critics, and he points to a host of theorists in the field who address diverse theoretical and political projects.
22. Francis Mulhern, "The Politics of Cultural Studies," journal title 47:3 (July 1995), pp. 31-40.
23. See Stanley Aronowitz, *The Politics of Identity,* especially the chapter "On Intellectuals," (New York: Routledge, 1992), pp. 125-174. Hall, "The Centrality of Culture," pp. 207-238.
24. Hall cited in Drew, "Cultural Composition," p. 183.
25. See Ian Hunter, *Rethinking the School* (New York: St. Martin's Press, 1994). This position is also argued for in Tony Bennett, "Out in the Open: Reflections on the History and Practice of Cultural Studies," *Cultural Studies* 10:1 (1996), pp. 133-153. A particularly telling but theoretically sloppy version of this position can be found in Maria Koundoura, "Multiculturalism or Multinationalism?" in David Bennett, ed., *Multicultural States* (New York: Routledge, 1998), pp. 69-87. Most of these critics appear to have little or no knowledge of the long history of debates within American educational circles over issues of reproduction, resistance, and the politics of schooling. Koundoura is especially uninformed on this issue, citing one article to defend her attack on "border pedagogy." For a review of the resistance literature, see Stanley Aronowitz and Henry A. Giroux, *Education Still Under Siege* (Westport, Conn.: Bergin and Garvey Press, 1994). An interesting critique of the work of Tony Bennett and Ian Hunter and the limits of governmentality as they apply it can be found in Toby Miller, *Technologies of Truth* (Minneapolis: University of Minnesota Press, 1998), and in Alan O'Shea, "A Special Relationship? Cultural Studies, Academia and Pedagogy," *Cultural Studies* 12:4 1998, pp. 513-527.
26. Alan O'Shea, "A Special Relationship?" Another challenge to the governmentality model can be found in the brilliant article on pedagogy and cultural studies by Richard Johnson, "Teaching Without Guarantees: Cultural Studies, Pedagogy and Identity," in Joyce Canaan and Debbie Epstein, eds., *A Question of Discipline* (Boulder, Colo.: Westview Press, 1997), pp. 42-73.
27. Stuart Hall, "Identity: Who Needs Identity?" p. 3.
28. Ibid., p. 4.
29. Hall, "The Centrality of Culture," p. 237.
30. Ibid., p. 232.
31. Hall, "Subjects in History," p. 289.
32. Hall et al., *Doing Cultural Studies,* p. 23.
33. Grossberg, "Cultural Studies," p. 248.
34. Hall, "Race, Culture, and Communications," p. 11.
35. One of the most incisive commentaries on the meaning and importance of Hall's theory of articulation can be found in Lawrence Grossberg, "On Postmodernism and Articulation: An Interview with Stuart Hall," *Journal of Communication Inquiry* 10:2 (Summer 1986), pp. 45-60.
36. Stuart Hall and David Held, "Citizens and Citizenship," in Stuart Hall and Martin Jacques, eds., *New Times: The Changing Face of Politics in the 1990s* (London: Verso, 1990), pp. 173-188.
37. Grossberg, "Cultural Studies," p. 259.
38. Herman Gray, *Watching Race* (Minneapolis: University of Minnesota Press, 1995), p. 132.

39. Hall, "Race, Culture and Communications," p. 11.
40. John Beverly, "Pedagogy and Subalternity: Mapping the Limits of Academic Knowledge," in Rolland G. Paulston, ed., *Social Cartography* (New York: Garland, 1996), p. 352.

INDEX

Henry, Jeffrey, 94
Heritage Foundation, 86
heroin chic, 68-81
heroin use, 70-3
Higonnet, Ann, 16
Hirsch, Jr., E. D., 111, 116-28, 131, 155
home as a safe place, 48
hope, politics of, 146-7
Hornsby, Andre J., 84
Hudson Institute, 86
Hunter, Ian, 163-4

I-D (magazine), 75, 77
Iggy Pop, 71
innocence, childhood 2, 61-2
    18th century idea of, 15
    ideal of, 9-10
    as moral ethos, 40
    myth of, 5-7, 39
    politics of, 5-15, 21-22
    protecting, 41
    rhetoric of, 21-22
innocence profiling, 7
intellectuals, 3, 134-6, 137, 140, 171
Internet, 12, 13, 15, 17, 30

Jane's Addiction, 70
Jawbreaker (film), 21
Jefferson, Thomas, 143
Jenkins, Henry, 5, 16, 30
Johnson, Richard, 3-4
Jones, Terry, 78
Joplin, Janis, 70

Kanka, Megan, 47
Kantrowitz, Barbara, 20
Katz, Jon, 30
Kearns, David, 86, 87
Kelley, Robin, 102
Kemp, Paula, 76
Kennedy, Edward, 41
Kid (film), 70
King, James, 77-8

King, Jr., Martin Luther, 105
Klaas, Polly, 47
Klebold, Dylan, 7, 8
Klein, Calvin. See Calvin Klein
knowledge production, 120-1
Kozol, Jonathan, 88

Labaree, David, 89
LaCour, V. J., 55
Landy, Marcia, 133
Life (magazine), 51-2
Lipsitz, George, 28
Littleton, Colorado. See Columbine High School, 1999 killings
Lott, Trent, 8

Macedo, Donaldo, 148
Madonna, 18
Males, Mike, 11, 23
Mann, Horace, 105, 143
Manning, Steven, 104-5
Marcuse, Herbert, 139
Mark, Ellen, 53
market culture, 1-2
Marston, Ginna, 73
Marx, Karl, 118, 124-5
Marxism, 109, 117, 147, 161
McDean, Craig, 76
McDonald Corporation, 95, 98
McGraw-Hill, 96
McMartin Preschool case (1987), 43
media, 7, 12, 17, 21, 30, 40, 49
Meier, Deborah, 102
Meisel, Steven, 68, 76, 77
Microsoft, 85
Milken, Michael, 85, 92-3
Miller, Lois, 55
Miss America beauty pageant, 58
Molnar, Alex, 100
Moss, Kate, 54, 60
motherhood, 9-10
Mulhern, Francis, 163
multiculturalism, 126
Mussolini, Benito, 109, 118, 131